Balancing Justice

Power, Politics, and Privilege

Phillip B. Bridgmon
John W. Clark III
University of North Alabama

KENDALL/HUNT PUBLISHING COMPANY
4050 Westmark Drive Dubuque, Iowa 52002

ISBN 0-7575-2609-8

Printed in the United States of America
10 9 8 7 6 5 4 3 2 1

Table of Contents

Tables and Figures

Tables

Figures

Acknowledgments

Since very little is ever accomplished without kindness and benevolence, it is a right and honorable measure to thank those who helped to make this project possible. We are thankful to our host institution, the University of North Alabama, for providing both financial support and a collegial environment for pursuing a book length manuscript. The staff at Kendall/Hunt has been true professionals at every turn, and we are thankful for the adroit skills and focused attention.

Phil Bridgmon and John Clark
University of North Alabama

To my wife Shannon who is the smartest, kindest, and funniest academic I know. She also is a veteran encourager of my work. She is supportive and inquisitive, and to me she is perfect.

Te Amo,
Phil

To Mom, Dad, John John and Casey,

Thanks for being a wonderful family.

Love always,
John

Preface

When one of us went through the doctoral program in political science, a professor would begin the first class with a discussion of what democracy means. By the end of the session we had hammered out ideas concerning free press, meaningful elections, one person/one vote, majority rule while protecting minority rights. After several classes with this ritual, the importance of clarifying certain aspects of governance began to crystallize. We feel this monograph provides a similar ritual.

In a recent issue of the Journal of Criminal Justice Education, Williams and Robinson (2004) assert that criminal justice lacks the perspective of ideology and politics that would give the discipline more rigor and respectability. Most scholars within criminal justice would agree that the discipline is a "recently emerged" area of study within the ivory tower. This emergence relies on and draws together bits and pieces of "more established" disciplines such as political science, psychology, public administration, economics, anthropology, sociology, and social work. By drawing from these academic tracks, criminal justice students gain an understanding of why crime occurs, its effects upon society as well as society's response to it. Thus, justice is meted out by individuals and institutions within an environment that influences the process.

While work on this monograph began before seeing the call by Williams and Robinson, we felt emboldened by the idea that our work could fill a small void for students of criminal justice. For us, politics touches everything meaningful in the social world in both good and bad aspects. By providing a sketch of the political environment of justice machinations and justice policies, students could then evaluate policies, practices, and the rhetoric of justice. Any course, for example, that deals with criminological theory and justice policy doesn't marry one another very well. The reason for this disjoint is largely attributable to the fact that justice is politicized.

No sinister undertones are meant by politicized justice. We contend that politics in most realms of policy and administration are natural and desired. Politics allows for popular control of government operations such as law enforcement, judicial process, and corrections. Without politics, citizens lose their ability to make demands and influence government. Very few individuals are willing to give up that right of a democracy even though they rarely and ineffectively exercise it.

Our approach begins from the assumption that most citizens are pleasantly detached from what government does including justice issues. We begin by detailing how politics influences justice and what the current result of that fact has come to mean to most conscientious observers. Essentially, we examine the idea of a dual system of justice one for those with means and one without. Anecdotal evidence points us toward justice system actors who have admitted their work is political and politicized. Given these combining forces, an elite theory of policy making that is rooted in wealth and ideology is developed. We then go on to examine justice policies and issues from these perspectives.

Students of criminal justice particularly, and justice more generally, will hopefully appreciate the attention to issues of politics, ideology, and wealth throughout the monograph. By understanding how these notions affect policies and administration of justice one can then look at any topic within justice and gain a richer understanding of its meaning to a free society. Just as courses in public opinion, political behavior, and social justice began with a core understanding of democracy, so should any course examining any aspect of justice. Hopefully, we have concisely provided such fodder.

Chapter One Introduction

"I am a political figure"[1]
William H. Pryor

Justice is a worthwhile pursuit. Roman philosophers placed justice at the pinnacle of society. Presidents seek justice during wars. Crime victims and their families want justice when it comes to those who have wronged them. Church billboards proclaim "Peace with justice," as if peace does not exist without it. Perhaps it should read "Peace can not be achieved without some form of justice." Students want justice when they perceive a slight during the handing out of grades. Historically oppressed minorities want justice in access to education and opportunities. Perspectives of what is justice are numerous. For the crime victim, a punishment of life in prison for the criminal offender may be justice. The state may believe justice is probation coupled with community service. Each party to an action brings different expectations as they relate

[1] In his confirmation hearing before the Senate Judiciary Committee on June 11, 2003, Judge Pryor was the Attorney General for the State of Alabama when he was appointed by President Bush to the Eleventh Circuit Court of Appeals in Atlanta, GA. Mr. Pryor's testimony before the committee elicited strong opposition from Democrats who perceived him as too conservative, ideological, and political. Colleagues at the state attorney general level viewed him as the most political attorney general in the United States. Nevertheless, he was passed out of committee on a party line vote, and became embroiled in a judicial confirmation tug of war between filibustering Democrats and the White House. Compromise by Senate moderates removed the filibuster threat only if the Republican leadership would not bring forth the most controversial nominees. Pryor was confirmed.

to the idea of justice. Perspectives of justice are dependent upon circumstance, context, and the need to resolve cognitive dissonance. Put another way, justice is sought and delivered from a number of stations, social classes, power imbalances, and political positions.

"I am a political figure"--the quote by William H. Pryor that began this chapter--epitomizes the work of those who toil in the field of criminal justice. Justice occupations, like Mr. Pryor's position as attorney general at the time of his appointment to the federal bench, are political occupations. Justice actors, such as police officers, chiefs, sheriffs, deputies, agents, probation officers, wardens, guards, judges, and state attorneys, occupy a place within the formal justice system whereby their responsibilities are legally prescribed and intentionally limited.[2] As these professionals go about their responsibilities, sworn to by most justice personnel, they are conditioned according to the human limits of the system. These limits are created by the environment in which public servants conduct their daily work. This environment shrouds and influences not only the resources that justice personnel will have for their work, but indirectly shapes the way that work is conducted. The criminal and civil justice systems are thus influenced by politics in ways that undermine many of the core values of the public sector and the pursuit of justice.[3]

---

[2] The roles and responsibilities of each component of the justice system—law enforcement, courts, corrections—have been viewed as an assembly line (Herbert Packer).

[3] Efficiency, effectiveness, equity, and economy are some of the core values of public work. The justice system in the United States, loosely construed, does not exhibit most of these values for any significant amount of time.

Politics Desired

We are not the first to assert that justice is influenced by politics. Martin Shapiro in (1964) asserted that "the core of political jurisprudence is a vision of courts as political agencies and judges as political actors."[4] James Q. Wilson, around the same time, posited that law enforcement's predominant policing style was shaped by the "local political culture."[5] Contemporary work that attempts to illuminate how the political environment influences the judicial process is vast and intriguing.[6] As a consequence, some very rich and compelling literature has developed concerning justice and politics.

At first glance, politics seems to be juxtaposed with justice. It is hard to find many people who react positively to either word. Many citizens view politics as a gritty business requiring too much compromise. They in turn view justice as a delicate balance that is rarely obtained. Inserting politics into the balancing act of justice can doom the pursuit of justice. Many believe justice is unattainable with any hint of politics. Simultaneously, while leery of both justice attainment and the craft of politics, citizens recognize that our justice systems do not behave according to normative notions of "equal treatment under the law" or "justice being blind" or those accused "being innocent until proven guilty." Yet, despite the

---

[4] Martin Shapiro (1964). "Political Jurisprudence", Kentucky Law Journal, 52, p. 294.

[5] James Q. Wilson (1968). Varieties of Police Behavior. Harvard University Press: NY.

[6] At the annual meeting of the Southwest Political Science Association (2005) a public law panel created a weblog to be hosted at LaGrange College in Georgia. Tracy Lightcap organized and secured resources so that a group of academics interested in how the judicial process runs its course could share ideas, brainstorm, and hopefully create synergies that lead to those incremental additions of knowledge to the subfield.

skepticism of both justice and politics there are no real reform efforts.[7]

We contend that justice permeated by politics, including the administration of justice, is desired by both elite and non-elite citizens. With politics, citizens believe that despite how the justice system actually works, they actually have some semblance of power to change it if they wanted. The alternative to politics would be a justice system absent of discretion, popularly influenced decisions, and managed by technocrats or experts. Thus, politics is a permanent fixture in the dispensing of justice. This iron law has consequences.

Dual Justice

During the summer we were finishing up this monograph several high profile trials ended in not guilty verdicts. Michael Jackson in a California court was absolved of all charges in a child sexual abuse case. In Alabama, Richard Scrushy--former HealthSouth leader--beat a fraud charge in a case that secured guilty pleas from all significant vice presidents who worked for him. In both of these acts of jury nullification, tremendous evidence of guilt was provided by the state in each case. The similarities in the Jackson and Scrushy cases don't stop there, however. Both gentlemen are wealthy and high profile members of their communities. In fairness to Jackson, he is known worldwide. Viewers of both trials were treated to defense strategies that can only be secured with resources: capable lawyers, theater-like atmospheres, experts, drama, and chicanery. After his arrest, but before trial, Scrushy hatched his own religious talk show, began guest preaching at predominately African-American churches, and donated generously to the religious community in Birmingham,

[7] Matthew Robinson (2004). Justice Blind. Prentice Hall. Upper Saddle River: NJ. Most reform is aimed at crating efficiencies with technology.

Alabama. Professional observers wrote extensively on the manipulation and the appearance that money and strategy overcame weak legal positions for both Scrushy and Jackson.

Roughly ten years preceding the Jackson and Scrushy verdicts, the O.J. Simpson trial featured a leading criminal defense "dream team" led by Johnnie Cochran, who at the time was defense attorney to the stars and avid loather of law enforcement. These cases reveal several important aspects of justice. One is the idea of celebrated cases. Celebrated cases are those crimes that are either heinous or rare or committed by media-worthy individuals. These cases make for good television. They draw in viewers and newspapers gain new readers. They don't tell us much about the justice system's day to day operations, however. In these cases, we see media attention heighten due to the status of the defendants and the role of money in securing "not guilty" verdicts. What can be gleaned from these cases is the basis for our justice system: justice is shaped by mass attention and ability and resources dictate success or failure within it. Jeffrey Reiman (2004) in his classic book describes the consequences of this fact as the "rich get richer and the poor get prison."[8]

An obvious question that arises is how does wealth and skill come to dominate the outcome of justice proceedings? We contend that the justice system is an open system that receives inputs from many different sources: justice personnel, victims, media, special interest groups, politicians, etc. In the quest to pacify the many divergent interests, each colored by politics and ideology, what emerges is a contest not between guilt and innocence but power, politics and privilege. By extension, if we view the justice system as a game as some scholars have, we can expect that those who are smarter, more

---

[8] Jeffrey Reiman (2004). The Rich Get Richer and The Poor Get Prison: Ideology, Class, and Criminal Justice. 7th (ed). Allyn and Bacon: Boston: MA.

observant, connected, and motivated will do better within the justice system than those who are dull, passive, marginalized, and distracted.[9]

In the realm of politics, money has come to dominate much of the work of government. Wealthy financiers fund campaigns and political parties. As a result, those who are elected represent a policy preference that is closely aligned with the benefactors of politicians. Lobbyists and interest groups also provide tangible resources to those who will give them their ear during the development of policies, rules, and regulations. We therefore logically connect the dots: money dominates politics, politics dominates justice, and money dominates justice. We further discuss this topic in chapter 2. Ultimately, we are all playing our prescribed role. Some are just in better position than others.

Plan of the Book

We have a few modest goals for this monograph. They should not be taken as priorities as we believe they all have some valuable contribution for justice. Our primary goal is to merge the ideas of politics, policy making, and the administration of justice with some behavior-oriented research on organizations. We treat issues related to the political environment, media, interest groups, and the underlying motivation of justice personnel. We hope to reveal how the political environment of public organizations shapes their work. By drawing together these strands of academic thought, perhaps students of justice can gain a better appreciation for the juggling act that our justice personnel do for their fellow citizens. If more citizens debated what justice means and how we can increase it because of this work, all would be good.

---

[9] See A. Bloomberg's "Confidence Game" and Laubman "Dual Legal Profession".

Chapter two sketches our theoretical assumptions concerning how justice policies are made, implemented, and evaluated. We borrow heavily from the work of Thomas Dye who advances a compelling theoretical argument for an elite driven policy process. Dye's arguments are coupled with Lindblom's assertion that policy is fragmented, ineffective, and slow to change due to the constraining limits of policy development. Toward the end of chapter two some specific policies are examined in order to demonstrate our theoretical assumptions.

Chapter three discusses the foundation for all human interaction, and the daily work of justice actors: discretion. Discretion is at the heart of any understanding of justice. It permeates the work and decision making of police officers, state prosecutors, judges, and correctional personnel. Discretion always leads to a "what if" as it relates to alternate choices of action. We simply don't have the knowledge as to which course of action is superior when discretion is exercised. What we do know is that discretion is used to promote personal agendas, curry favor with the powerful, and often undermines justice.

Chapter four details how law enforcement is not immune to political pressures. This chapter sketches the political environment of law enforcement by using several media cases concerning police corruption, abuse of power, and racial profiling. In addition, a historical placement of the police within a Constitutional society is explored. We also look at some recent trends toward hiring and the socialization of law enforcement actors.

The politics of the judiciary are examined in chapter five. We cover the scholarship on judicial decision making to highlight the idea of "political jurisprudence." Our focus is aimed primarily at the United States Supreme Court, but we also examine sub-national courts, methods of selecting judges, and the implications that arise from different methods of selection and different models of decision making. Chapter five concludes with some anecdotal evidence that supports the fact that courts have not always been the arbiter of fairness when bowing to political pressures.

In chapter six, we further examine how rights of the accused are often politicized through infringements upon civil liberties and the slow chipping away of Constitutional guarantees through the practice of law. We delve into the consequences of an over reliance on plea bargaining, public defenders, and erratic protections given by a trial by jury.

Chapter seven begins our focus on politicized punishment. Our prisons are full of non-violent inmates who are incarcerated because punishment is politicized. There exist alternatives to traditional punishment and a more comprehensive range of punishments that could serve society. We rarely hear about these in public debates. Our examination looks at the consequences of this void.

Death is the ultimate punishment and is covered in detail in chapter eight. Most states in the United States have an active death penalty system. We acknowledge there is a great call for using this punishment. In contrast, a person who resists this form of punishment is accused of being soft on crime. The most enduring fact of the death penalty is that it historically has been applied in a discriminatory manner against people of color, lower incomes, and those with low intelligence levels. We have also executed innocent individuals. This happens when our appetite for vengeance overrides our ability to rationally apply punishments that equally serve the only purpose death penalty advocates champion: incapacitation.

Chapter nine attempts to offer balance to our coverage of criminal law as we look at an area of politicized civil law: the politics of tort reform. We contend that tort justice is more politicized than any other justice issue. Advocates of tort reform count liberals, conservatives, Presidents, regular citizens, business types, and consumers as teammates in the effort to make it more difficult for those harmed by others to seek redress in the courts. States have been successful in reforming their tort laws in the name of being friendly to business. Most recently, the federal government reformed class action lawsuits, and is moving toward limiting tort cases arising from years of damaging asbestos usage.

Guiding Ideas

We contend that politics drives justice policies and justice administration. This has led to some shortcomings in the justice system. It is important to keep in mind that while politics is sometimes dirty, irresponsible, and irrational; the alternative is not amenable to us or most citizens. Every now and then politics can lead to compromise and accommodation that was previously not possible. Knowing how politics shapes our world gives us the ability to anticipate it, work within a political system, and create the best possible conditions for success. Justice depends on it.

Chapter Two Justice and the Policy Process

Government's response to crime (public wrongs) and private wrongs fall within a broad construct that can be called justice policy. What governments decide to do or not do can be defined as public policy. This definition has both positive and negative aspects. It involves both an overt response and action by government, but policy can also developed by inaction on the part of government. Justice policies thus become value statements, and the implementation of them can also be value laden. For example, if we pass laws that make carrying a weapon to school illegal we are saying more about our views of where carrying a weapon is appropriate. If law enforcement does not enforce such a rule, that too becomes an expression of a societal value.[1]

Justice Defined

Justice is an elusive concept that conjures up notions of punishment, reward, and equity of the process that produces both rewards and punishments. We may think of justice as doing what is right, morally correct, and fair. Justice can be both real and imagined in the eye of the beholder which necessitates that justice be subjective. According to John Rawls (1971), justice can be achieved through appropriate processes whereby governments make decisions that promote

[1] The right to carry a weapon on school grounds seems like a settled issue. However, school districts are struggling to enforce zero tolerance policies as they relate to weapons. In Harrisonburg, VA, for example, bans on the possession of weapons on school grounds ran afoul of state law. Apparently, both safety advocates and gun advocates have found worthy foes in this debate.

equity and strengthen the social contract.[2] Much of Rawls's theory hinges upon society cloaking itself in what he calls a "veil of ignorance." While cloaked, any individual is unaware of his or her intelligence, station, infirmity, or needs. If asked to distribute public goods, like justice, wealth, and opportunity, we could make these decisions without any assurance of who will benefit from them. Rawls asserts that we would be more likely to distribute these public benefits more equitably than they now are, thus yielding justice.

Rawls' theory of justice is important to our discussion due to his focus on process. We contend that justice policies and the administration of justice take place within an environment that does not promote justice either through process or as an initial goal. Our assertion is not an indictment of the many fine and respectable members of the criminal and civil justice systems. Since we do not make public decisions cloaked in ignorance, there are no guarantees that the work of law enforcement officers, judges, attorneys, or corrections personnel will always be made with justice as the primary beneficiary. To behave justly is ephemeral. Whether or not this helps to achieve justice broadly and at acceptable levels are relative.

Politics and Policy

Scholars have developed a number of systematic methods for viewing public policy.[3] Since justice policy is a public policy,

---

[2] John Rawls (1971). A Theory of Justice. Harvard University Press: Cambridge, MA.

[3] There are a number of books dedicated to how public policy works. Policy analysis, as a term developed to include all of the aspects of policy, owes a debt to many disciplines such as economics (game theory), as well as traditional policy studies within the field of political science. While there are a number of equally competitive explanations of the policy process, we tend to lean more heavily on Dye's elaboration of the elite

their frameworks highlight the important components of justice policies, and the important aspects of policy analysis that are neglected. Any policy can be examined in roughly three ways: process, content, and evaluation. The policy process falls under the auspices of models of politics, for which there are at least a dozen. Content, or what a policy does, is descriptive and normative. Evaluation wrestles with the "so what" question of whether or not a policy prescription makes a significant difference in nature of the public problem it was supposed to address.

Regardless of which theoretical framework is adopted, all of them have in common the idea that politics matters. Since little attention has been paid to the idea that politics matters, a void exists for understanding justice policies on one hand, and the results we get for our investments in the justice system on the other. Thus, politics and the political environment are integral to this examination (See Figure 2-1).

Figure 2-1: The Environment of Justice

Media
Citizens
Interest Groups → Justice Actors-→ JUSTICE or INJUSTICE?
Victims Justice Process

Our examination pays special attention to the political environment and attempts to bring the study of justice issues within the confines of more traditional studies of politics and policies. Thus, we attempt to determine the precise role politics plays in the distribution of justice. Does politics undermine justice or is it a prerequisite for justice? First and

---

theory, Stone's brilliant work on the art of political decision making, and Lindblom's reminder that much of what we do is still muddling through, at best.

foremost, it is important to divulge our assumptions and working definitions of politics as well as our general framework. We have no axe to grind, or political statement to make with this work. The goals of our examination are to determine if we are amenable to the importance of politics in justice systems, and the desirability of maintaining such a system.

Politics is the means by which members of a society resolve conflicts without physically harming one another.[4] Students of politics will immediately jump at this notion of politics because the resolution of political conflict usually ends with one side diminished or outright harmed. While this could be the case, politics is a process that involves the utilization of formal institutions, personal relationships, and external pressures, such as the media, and sometimes power. When politics plays out in a traditional perspective we can envision it, as some have suggested, as a good thing.[5]

Politics is necessary due to the scarcity of public goods. Since there exists more demand for public goods—education, road building, protection, tax code preferences, government contracts—than resources to provide them, the competition for them includes both conflict and compromise.[6] This essence has been captured nicely by E. E. Schattschneider who describes politics as a fight (conflict) and Harold Laswell who appropriately described politics as determining who gets what.[7] Politics yields winners and losers. During the process,

---

[4] Carl von Clausewitz is an exception in that he also viewed war as a "continuation of politics by other means."

[5] Larry Sabato at the University of Virginia is often quoted on political matters and routinely refers to politics as a good thing.

[6] Gary Jacobson & Samuel Kernell (2004). Logic of American Politics, CQ Press: Washington, D.C.

[7] E.E. Schattscheider (1970).The Semisoverign People. Dryden Press, Hinsdale, IL. Harold Laswell (1958). Politics, Who Gets What, When, and How. McGraw Hill, NY:NY.

some actors achieve their goals while others must wait their turn or recalibrate their tactics and goals. We view justice personnel as political actors who make daily decisions concerning the distribution of public goods. These actors must also respond and work within a larger environment as outlined in Figure 2-1. Thus, they carry out day-to-day responsibilities as part of a broader environment that requires them to maintain complex relationships that may or may not undermine justice. This broader environment is largely shaped and managed by elite actors such as elected officials, the media, and moneyed interests.

Elite Politics

Our assumption concerning who are the most important political actors in the development of justice policies is rooted in an elite theory of policy making.[8] Thomas Dye is probably the most well known author associated with the elite model. He contends that all aspects of policy analysis, including development and evaluation, are controlled by elite actors drawn primarily from moneyed interests. The elite model contains several prevailing assumptions, some agreeable to us, that must be highlighted before analyzing Dye's theoretical construct.

Elite politics is seen as promoting the preferences of governing elite. The term elite means few; they occupy a small space at the top of the model. In the center of the model are those who monitor and actually do the work of government. They can be thought of as elected officials and government administrators. The largest segment of the model is all others, which include low level bureaucrats and average citizens (see Figure 2-2).

---

[8] The most lucid discussion of policy making from a top-down approach is Thomas Dye (2002). Top-Down Policy Making. Chatham House: NY:NY.

Figure 2-2: Model of Elite Theory

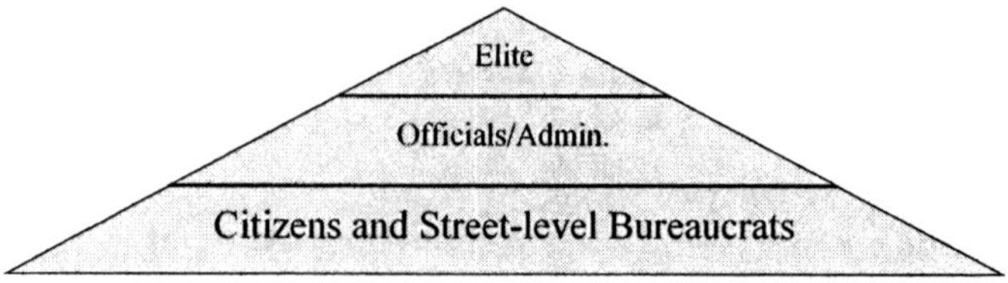

The elite theory of politics is based upon several assumptions. All theoretical models make some assumptions that can be compared and contrasted, which we will do later in the chapter.

1. In any society, there will only be a few who have power. Average citizens are not part of the policy making apparatus.
2. The governing elite are drawn from the wealthy.
3. Movement in and out of the governing elite is rigid, ordered, and slow.
4. Elites seek to maintain their power by promoting and protecting adopted values on behalf of average citizens: protection of property, limited government, and liberty.
5. Policies are not based on the preference of average citizens. Policy changes occur incrementally.
6. Iron Law of Oligarchy—active elite (minority) will always control an apathetic majority.[9]

[9] See supra note 1.

If true, some of the assumptions of the elite theory can be troubling for many citizens to accept. In most democratic societies, the notion of concentrated power is contrary to the idea of self determination and governance. Much governing in the United States does occur by a small group of people, whether elected officials, former elected officials, Washington, D.C. based think-tanks, interest groups, law firms, or corporate interests.[10]

Another assumption worth touching upon is the idea of incremental changes in policy. If elites seek to protect their power, and make decisions based on a set of shared values, then their efforts must be centered on a policy process that is slow and at times unwieldy. The term used by scholars is "incremental change."[11] Policy is developed piece by piece. Changes take place from year to year, and even then, radical policy development is not the norm. Debates concerning any single policy area usually centers on whether or not funding should be increased or decreased. Once government decides to dedicate appropriations to an activity, it's difficult to reverse such a decision. You may have heard it put this way: "There is no such thing as a temporary government program." This absolute statement is wrong, of course. Programs end, change, and begin often. What doesn't change is that government grows ever so slightly each year. It does so at the behest of the ruling elite.

We can not ignore the final assumption of an Iron Law of Oligarchy. Even if the other assumptions of elite policy making are not valid, the assumption that the active few will always lead the passive masses is difficult to discount. While we don't deal with "laws" very often in the social sciences, anecdotal evidence from your own work in organizations may

---

[10] Id.

[11] Charles Lindblom (1968). The Policy-Making Process. Prentice Hall: NJ.

be convincing enough to show that a handful of individuals usually end up completing most organizational tasks. Here, the task we are referring to is setting an agenda and engaging in the pursuit of that agenda or making policy.

Neither of us asserts that the elite or active minority have sinister intentions. Their power and position is largely achieved by default. Explaining how the elite become the elite, or maintain their status, is a function of interest, abilities, and attitude.[12] On the whole, not everyone has an interest in government and politics. The work of government is seen as secondary to livelihood and happiness. Essentially, then, society can be divided into two groups: those with the ability to govern and those who are fit to be governed. We primarily take our focus from this point and examine the behavior of those who govern to determine if their decisions can be improved and by extension, foster a sense of justice.

Incrementalism

We have already mentioned that policy change in the United States occurs slowly. Regardless of which model of politics one uses, the rate of change will be fairly constant. Governments only move swiftly on policy problems when forced to or when mass public opinion leaves them no option. Most recently, Congress moved in less than a week to tighten up restrictions on telemarketers, and attempted to do so in the sensationalized case of Terri Shiavo.[13] Neither example

---

[12] Some well known conservative scholarship in this area is Walter Lippman and Ed Banfield. Lippman, for example, asserts that the masses are not fit to govern. Banfield, noted for his work on attitude and individual success, would point toward an individual's outlook and perspective rather than their connections, wealth, family upbringing, etc.

[13] Terri Schiavo remained in a vegetative state for 18 years before succumbing to death. Her husband's decision to remove her feeding tube and IV caused a jolt to the right to live movement, and prompted Florida's

drastically changed the course of government or policy toward phone calls at home or right to die legislation. They were individualistic and narrow policies. On most matters, politic or governmental bodies move deliberately.

The ability of government to move quickly on most policy issues is hampered by several basic fundamentals: structure, politics, time, and information. The Founding Fathers viewed a system of government that was careful, limited, and inefficient as compatible with the elite values of life, liberty, and sanctity of property.[14] Most citizens also contend that a slow, inefficient government that allows for some input is superior to one administered by "experts" not under the control of popular sentiment. Others would contend that we need a blend of popular control and harnessed expertise to achieve the public good. We agree there exist a blend, but not on a wide scale. It is also important to note that rational and efficient government is in juxtaposition to a government that must respond to transparent and changing political demands.

For all legislative bodies, time is a critical factor in determining agenda items and the degree to which policy can be altered. Legislative sessions are mandated typically by law. These representative bodies can only meet for so long, and

---

governor Jeb Bush, and the Republican Congress to seek an injunction to save Schiavo's life. Their efforts ran up against both the Constitution of Florida and the United States. This is an example, however, of the machinations of government not always being slow and unresponsive.

[14] For a compelling argument for our system of government, the Federalist Papers by James Madison, Alexander Hamilton, and John Jay make the strongest case for its virtues. Mostly written by Madison, the Federalist Papers are a must for students of policy, public administration, and politics. Also, the Madisonian dilemma was Madison's concern that an active majority could trample a helpless minority. Or, how best to structure a government that allows the "majority" rule but protects minority rights? The U.S. Constitution with the first 10 Amendments became the remedy to his dilemma.

their business follows a set of rules that make the process predictable and workable for what are large bodies of decision makers. The politics of process also slows down the work of government. Competition exists over setting the agenda, hearings take time, markup (writing the bill), and votes (many are procedural) have to be scheduled. Days off for meetings don't allow every day of the session to be dedicated to voting on policy. Time limits hinder the ability of government to address every policy problem in a thorough way.

Even if governments had unlimited time, they would still be short two important components of any decision: the available alternatives to any particular decision and the potential consequences of the action. These ultimately preclude governments from making rational choices among competing courses of action, and undermine the adequacy of policy responses to public problems. We do not contend that these are the goals of government action. They are pointed out here because political rhetoric would lead a casual observer to conclude that policies are developed as real solutions that ultimately solve and rid society of whatever problem the policy was created to address.[15]

The politics of the policy process create fierce competition over scarce resources. Political maneuvering, combined with the structure of political decision making, also slows the pace at which policy can be changed. For example, the filibuster is a long held parliamentary tactic known as talking a bill to death. As a political technique, users of the

[15] Charles Lindblom called this process muddling through. Muddling, in the realm of policy deliberations, is akin to a fish being out of water. It conjures up a flailing about. Sometimes government gets it right, other times they don't. Stone contends that this ultimately leads to the "paradox" of policy. On the one side it is supposed to solve problems and protect citizens, yet policies are deficient due to the political nature of decision making which includes strategies, withholding complete information, distortion, and chicanery.

filibuster may actually be able to talk a bill (policy change) to death, but they can highlight its importance and may be able to get some concessions regarding small changes to the overall legislation. Politics may involve media strategies that drum up support or opposition for a particular policy. In the current information age, technology has been used to circulate e-petitions, as well as to lobby Congress and spread political messages calling for action. The old phrase "talk is cheap" is very real. The more policy responses are talked about, debated, investigated, and researched, the less time for adopting solutions and implementing them. Our desire to maintain a political game creates a slowly moving, and hobbled decision-making apparatus.

Finally, governments are structured to proceed slowly. Unlike private enterprise, authority is statutorily prescribed. Decisions by government officials are vested in the hands of a very few, unless they allocate discretion to administrators.[16] The ability to meet and make decisions fall under open meeting laws. Community members must be notified, the press can attend, and written records of proceedings must be kept. Changing policies must be agreed upon by large numbers, coalitions must be developed, and mandated processes followed. In a system of checks and balances, any

[16] Administrative rules carry the weight of law and are created through an administrative process that adheres to the common justice principles of due process. Many legislative bodies create vague laws, and leave the specific application to government agencies. These agency decisions fall under the purview of administrative discretion, not legislative. Often, legislative preference and administrative preference are not synchronized. This leads to the legislative body exerting more influence and control over the policy specifics. Executive orders, over the years, have made it ore difficult to create administrative rules. Some require impact statements, justification, comment periods, and expensive environmental analysis. The message is simple: administrative rule making should be limited and fall under the purview of the desires of significant policy making bodies.

changes must be acceptable to both the executive and judicial branches. For example, the President may veto legislation and the courts can rule a law unconstitutional. Following the process, abiding by the rules, and getting others to agree is daunting and excruciatingly slow. We probably would like to have it otherwise.[17]

Justice Policy

From the perspective of elite and incremental policy making, we can now examine a significant justice policy to demonstrate how it came to be a policy, changed, and whether or not it has been successful. There are a number of policy areas to choose from, but we want to briefly examine the war on drugs. It permits a look at the particular public problem, the organized interests, policy content, and evaluation components associated with fighting illegal drugs.

War on Drugs

In the United States, policy makers have maintained an infatuation with addressing the non-medical use of drugs. To be sure, citizens of the United States consume a disproportionate amount of the globe's illicit drugs. The consequences of our prevalence rates are that we prop up governments that benefit from the illegal drug trade, undermine public health, and fray delicate social bonds. As a consequence, the full weight of law and efforts against drugs and terrorism burdens our justice system and costs billions of dollars each year. In short, we have a drug problem that

[17] Early in the presidency of George W. Bush, he made the public comment that governing would surely be a lot easier if we operated under a dictatorship. His statement is an explicit acknowledgement that change is slow and frustrating.

undermines the quality of our public health and safety, and we spend a disproportionate amount of money waging war on the possession of illegal drugs. Our war on drugs has not yielded the results our policy makers promised.

The war on drugs is not a recent war. Bertram and her colleagues classify our drug control efforts into at least three categories or paradigms beginning in (1900) with the punitive paradigm.[18] Past efforts at reducing drug usage have ranged from the mundane to the insane. For example, only two amendments of the United States Constitution deal with policy questions: prohibition of alcohol. One amendment prohibited alcohol sales, the other repealed the prohibition. Organized crime was the unintended consequence of the prohibition era, and our drug policies are a story of unintended consequences. The United States war on drugs has done nothing to limit the availability of drugs, alter the price, or the demand. Each of these is very worthwhile, specific, and measurable goals of our efforts against drugs. Like prohibition, the stigma of illegal drugs never materialized and the policies aimed at reducing drug usage and its ill effects have been proven deficient. If this is the case, and compelling evidence does indeed exist, where have policy makers gone wrong? Are the organized interests associated with this issue offering viable alternatives? Who are the major stakeholders? Can we improve our efforts related to curbing drug usage?
Chapter seven examines this issue further.

History

Much of the public's perception about our drug wars are shaped by the U.S. Presidency. Despite a history of legislation

---

[18] Eva Bertram, Morris Blachman, Kenneth Sharpe & Peter Andreas (1996). Drug War Politics: The Price of Denial. U.C.L.A. Press: Los Angeles, CA.

limiting the acquisition of drugs, it wasn't until Richard Nixon called the problem a national threat that the U.S. began a significant push to combat the use of illicit drugs.[19] Nixon's efforts to highlight illegal drug usage accomplished a bit more than bringing to bear the weight of the U.S. government on this issue. By 1970, with the passage of the Drug Abuse Prevention and Control Act, the usage of the bully pulpit by President Nixon had accomplished several significant milestones in the war on drugs. Most importantly, the general public was now aware of illicit drug usage, they had made the connection between drug usage and crime, and a broad war both domestically and foreign had been initiated.[20]

Over the past 35 years since Nixon's escalation of the war on drugs, presidents have tried to modify their policies according to their own ideology. President's Reagan and Bush maintained Nixon's get tough approach. Both presided over expanded efforts at interdiction, source control, and treatment programs. Law enforcement resources committed to fighting drugs also increased significantly under their watch, but with only negligible success. Total spending on combating drugs at the federal, state, and local levels is over $30 billion per year.[21]

Despite an effort to wage the war on drugs at a lower pitch, the presidency of Bill Clinton also included an expansion of resources dedicated to combating drugs, building and maintaining prisons, and expanding treatment efforts.[22] During the decade of the 1990's, the U.S. maintained a full-speed effort at waging the war on drugs. Some of the war is

---

[19] Id.
[20] Id.
[21] National Research Council, National Academy of Sciences, "Informing America's Policy on Illegal Drugs: What We Don't Know Keeps Hurting Us" (Washington, DC: National Academy Press, 2001), p. 1.
[22] See supra note 18.

based on fact, but most has been waged on myth. The war's costs have probably not produced the corresponding benefits. Some have concluded that our drug war history has taken a perverse toll.[23]

Problems

This very rich and thoroughly documented history with the United State's war on drugs leads to the obvious query as to why such a defunct effort can be maintained when the costs of the status quo are too high. James Gray's treatise on why our drug laws have failed and what can do about puts a fine point on some alternatives to the get tough mantra.[24]

Our drug policies have failed due to simple economics. Engaging in the sale, distribution and manufacture of illegal drugs is profitable. Nothing the justice system does can sufficiently increase the costs of participating in the drug trade. In fact, the war on drugs has probably increased profitability of the illegal drug trade. As profits increase, and demand stays level, the number of sources that supply drugs will increase in a corresponding manner.[25]

At another level, treatment programs, without a doubt, help individuals combat their cravings for drugs. Whether treatment is taken in an institutional setting or community program, participants are less likely to reuse, recommit crime, and be reconvicted. The problem with treatment is that it is often ordered too late to help, and the individualized aspects that point to success are rarely addressed. Treatment is also

---

[23] David Courtwright (1996). The Drug War's Perverse Toll, Issues in Science and Technology, Online: http://www.issues.org/issues/13.2/courtw.htm

[24] James Gray (2001). Why Our Drug Laws Have Failed And What We Can Do About It: A Judicial Indictment of the War on Drugs, Temple University Press, Philadelphia, PA.

[25] See supra note 18.

seen as being lenient and does not fit well with political rhetoric. The U.S. does not have a strong commitment to reducing demand for drugs through treatment.

This lack of commitment is the primary problem in the war on drugs. Scholars allude to the fundamental problem as a sense of denial on the part of lawmakers.[26] Politicians maintain a healthy denial because they benefit by using the same old and tired language to describe drugs. Even after independent government analysis reveals that the war on drugs has not worked, the push to get tough and do more of the same continues. The inattentive public rarely is presented with objective analyses concerning the war on drugs. They probably don't need to see the results of a study to know that the drug usage in the communities is at catastrophic levels. They see the carnage from illicit drug usage. Grandparents raising their grandchildren because their own children have been lost to drugs can tell the story. Washed out methamphetamine users who are unable to get and keep a steady job can paint the picture. Employers who have trouble finding non drug users know the results of our war on drugs. Our overworked and underpaid law enforcement personnel haven't seen their work decreased. Judges, some of who have given up and decided to publicly state that we are in denial, would show you their docket filled with drug and drug related crime.

Interests and What to Do Next

It is fairly easy to see that our drug policies are controlled by the governing elites. Congress began the movement to address illicit drug usage, and that effort was picked up by President Richard Nixon. The media age has only served to heighten the

[26] The sense of denial may be a conscious effort, but it does very little to help craft better drug control policies.

efforts of governing elites by allowing them to easily broadcast their messages to a mass audience. The war on drugs is not institutionalized by our law enforcement agencies at all levels of government. Each of these constitutes an elite component of the policy making apparatus according to Thomas Dye. All of the messages, communications, dissemination of facts, and discussion of illicit drug usage is aimed at keeping the war on drugs in its current direction.

Any changes in the policies toward illicit drugs will originate with the governing elite. Since many of these policies are aimed at protecting wealth and the governing power structure, it is unlikely that significant changes will occur despite the overwhelming evidence that the war on drugs is not working. The public will not be able to create change; policy change in an elite system flows downward not upward. At best, the U.S. citizenry may see incremental changes that tweak the war on drugs. What could be done differently in the war on drugs is worth examining briefly to determine why it won't occur? Gray has proffered several recommendations and suggestions that could result in a significant reorienting of our drug control policies.[27]

> Education—serious education programs about drugs including honesty and sincerity.
> Needle Exchange—implement on a wide scale to enhance the public health benefit.
> End Subsidies---it is a bit hypocritical for the government to sue tobacco companies for manufacturing a legal substance and also subsidizing its manufacturer.
> Medical Marijuana—some places have it, but the stigma still persists.

---

[27] See supra note 24 at pp. 240-245.

Hemp—grow it to save trees, create jobs, which was done during WWII
Community Policing—community policing requires a philosophical shift from traditional law enforcement to one that fosters citizen participation in the police process.
Drug Treatment—it has been shown to work in both community and institutional settings.
Expand Drug Courts—applies expertise and weight of sanctions to non-violent drug offenders. Gives them the help needed to be drug and crime free.
Change Budget Priorities—focus on programs not information.
Prisons—stop building them for the purpose of housing drug offenders.
Legal Drugs—the two most addictive and abused drugs are alcohol and tobacco, prescription drug abuse is a significant problem, too.
State Control—give states the resources and autonomy to create their own strategies to combat the drug problem.

Cut Out The Politics?

These suggestions are not new, but would require agreement from both major political parties, and across the ideological spectrum. Gray also spells out other suggestions not mentioned here; the bulk of the suggestions essentially are doing what works versus what sounds good.

Changing our direction in the war on drugs undermines the special interests. The war on drugs is permanently ingrained in our justice system, even though it is a fight that will not result in a victory.

Summary

Justice policies are created and maintained by governing elite whose primary interest is growing the economy and preserving power, not developing thoughtful and utilitarian responses to public problems. Our justice policies have very little to do with fostering justice or diminishing the consequences of crime. These policies are also developed incrementally, and in response to a growing awareness rather than through a proactive approach that may foster justice on several fronts such as social justice, economic justice, or environmental justice.

The consequences of justice policy development are most important to the citizens and dedicated public servants who work in the justice system. For it is the citizen who must finance the system while enjoying limited promotion of the public good, and the bureaucrat who toils daily in a conveyor system of justice that never sees a retooling or finished product. Our justice system simply recycles offenders.

Due to the nature of politics, the competing demands, and the lack of consensus on what constitutes justice and the public good, we are likely to see a continuation of current justice policies even though they have proven to be deficient. Responsive policies include building more prisons, hiring more guards, officers, border personnel, judges, and administrators. These policies will not be aimed at promoting justice and thoughtful policies, but will be undertaken because being tough on something is more politically attractive than being smart, right, or thoughtful.

We can examine the suggestions by Judge James Gray, which were outlined above, and see precisely where each of them would be found wanting. Some of the suggestions are indeed in place, but none are prevailing national policy. Some would appeal to those on the left, while others appeal to those on the right side of the ideological spectrum. None would be acceptable to even a plurality.

As we move along in our struggle to promote justice, it will continue to be relegated to a secondary issue in the face of more significant public problems such as terrorism. The glaring paradox here is that fighting terrorism is a fight for justice. Through our incremental and elite driven policies, we often lose sight of the real issues involved with our policy responses. Losing sight of the real issues hinders our ability to address these deficiencies.[28]

[28] Senator Howell Heflin, D-AL, was famous for his work in the area of jurisprudence. He served as Chief Justice of the Alabama Supreme Court before becoming a U.S. Senator. His personal approach to public policy was to gather the facts and always keep in mind the issue.

Chapter Three Discretion and Justice

Justice systems are constructed, managed, and staffed by humans. The boundaries of any justice system include those who process cases and those who are processed. Since it is people who are most affected by the justice system—citizens, attorneys, judges, victims, criminals—it is important to understand that justice can be politicized. Discretion involves the use of judgment when several courses of action are available. The use and exercise of justice hinders justice. It is also a requisite for the delivery of justice. In this chapter, discretion is discussed within the context of some significant justice actors: law enforcement, state attorneys, and judges. Most students of justice readily concede that judges routinely use discretion, but many are less familiar with those of law enforcement, prosecutors, and those in corrections. Through their discretionary roles, each has as much leverage in the justice system as do judges. By examining each discretionary role we can see when politics may penetrate the decisions of those charged with upholding the law and ensuring fair and equitable treatment under the law.

Discretion

Discretionary roles are inherent to the justice system. Indeed it is an a priori assumption on our part that discretion is a desirable tool in the dispensation of justice. Without discretion, imagine what our justice system would become? Law enforcement would be required to pursue full enforcement of the law. Every violation of the law reported or witnessed could result in arrest. If prosecuting attorneys ignored their political role and pursued every case filed with their office, our court dockets would be more clogged. Judges, if forced to exact maximum punishments, would soon feel the repercussions of a corrections system more in crisis.[1] The citizenry would probably protest as they would feel not only harassed by a heavy handed justice system, but also the financial brunt for paying the costs associated with a zero tolerance criminal justice system.

Discretion allows our justice system to find a steady equilibrium between the extreme of lax law enforcement and strict law enforcement. One of the goals of the justice system, in a normative sense, is to be a seamless component of society. That is to say, those citizens should be able to freely engage one another, so long as they are obeying the law, without significant interactions with the justice system. The way this manifests itself is quite simple. Citizens often desire to see a police car. When they call for service, they want it quickly. Prosecutors, through the course of their work, must demonstrate fairness and a willingness to take *serious* crimes *seriously*. Judges play a respected role that places them at the pinnacle of the justice system. When the various actors in the justice system move their behavior to the extreme opposite of what has been described here, the justice system ceases to be a seamless part of society and in turn manifest as an abrasion that wears on the unity of the community.

Knowing when to exercise discretion is a significant talent. Given the political nature of justice and the rigors of criminal justice work, many justice actors may never fully develop the right equilibrium in exercising discretion.[2]

---

[1] William Selke (1993). Prisons in Crisis. Indiana University Press: Bloomington:IN.

[2] Much has been written on the rigors of law enforcement, for example. Politically, judges and prosecutors seek office and sometimes lose. One of the distinguishing factors of the public sector is that leadership does turn over at a faster rate than in the private sector. This turn over creates disruptions, makes planning more difficult, and changes priorities. Popular control of government may hinder the equal application of justice.

Nevertheless, a significant amount of work has been invested in understanding when actors in the justice system exercise discretion, for what purpose, and to what effect that exercise of discretion has for the delivery of justice. Our attention now turns to the work of law enforcement, judges, and prosecutors.

Law Enforcement

Police in the United States occupy a special place within the justice system. They are the most recognizable aspect of the justice system.[3] Furthermore, within the U.S. system of constitutionally prescribed civil liberties, police arrest powers butt up against the freedom many U.S. citizens enjoy. Officers have been granted the authority to oppress and use force if necessary in the discharge of their duties.[4] This special role takes on significant meaning outside the consideration of discretion. Coercion and force are significant tools available to police officers. Coupled with the ability to use discretion in the meting out of arrest powers, law enforcement officers occupy a special place in the delivery of justice.

The level of research on police use of discretion mirrors the importance of the issue. As such, a multitude of literature reviews have developed the treat the use of discretion in law enforcement.[5] Most of the explanations of the use of discretion revolve around context of crime and officer

---

[3] Police officers are considered street level bureaucrats. Their occupational place would be akin to social workers, teachers, nurses, fire fighters, etc. See Lipsy in Shafritz & Hyde (2003), Classics of Public Administration, Thomson: NY.

[4] For discussions of use of force and roles of officers, Packer, The Limits of Criminal Sanction, Stanford University Press: CA; Reiss, 1971, The Police and the Public, Yale University Press: CT.

[5] Goldstein, in Cole, Gertz, and Bunger: The Criminal Justice System: Politics and Policies; Dunham and Alpert, (2005) Critical Issues in Policing, Waveland Press: IL.

characteristics/attitudes. Strangely, politics is a noticeable omission in the explanation of police use of discretion. However, our discussion does not end here. By examining what is known to affect discretion, we can then place politics as an explanation in its proper place.

Discretion has been linked to the level of bureaucratic sophistication of law enforcement agencies.[6] It is theorized that agencies with clearly outlined rules, responsibilities and training, lessen the probability that an individual within the organization will engage in discretionary behavior. Many observers of discretion and bureaucracy commingle discipline and chain of command as bureaucratic aspects while ignoring the more basic tenets such as professionalism.[7] Officers in well-run organizations, this includes adequate training and education and information sharing, will view their work differently than officers in other departments. As such, their opportunities for discretion are lessened, and their approach to police work will be with a stricter adherence to statutory laws and agency policies and procedures.

---

[6] Bittner (1970) The Functions of Police in Modern Society, NIH: MD.
[7] Some examples of structure, order, and discipline research are Bittner note 6; Skolnick (1966) Justice Without Trial: Law Enforcement in Democratic Society, John Wiley: NY; Manning (1977), Police Work: The Social Organization of Policing, MIT Press: MA; McNamara (1967) Uncertainties in Police Work" the Relevance of Police Recruits' Backgrounds and Training, in The Police: Six Sociological Essays by Bordua, Wiley: NY; 1977. Those who focus on professionalism include Goldstein (1977) Policing a Free Society, Harvard University Press: MA; Smith and Klein (1984) Police Control of Interpersonal Dispute, Social Problems, 31(4) pp167-78; Swanson (1978)"The Influence of Organization and Environment on Arrest Policies in Major U.S. Cities, Policy Studies Journal, v7: pp.390-418;. Smith (1984), The Organizational Aspects of legal Control, Criminology, 22 pp19-28 created a matrix for examining agencies based on one of four models—legalistic, militaristic, service, and fraternal departments.

Police work does not occur at the station, however. Police officers are highly visible public servants. Their work is shaped by their coworkers, supervisors, and citizens. As such, police discretion has been linked to what is broadly construed as neighborhood variables.[8] Neighborhood variables are the prevailing socio-economic status of a community: race, age, gender, class, education. Research on how these variables impact discretion typically centers on some weak tautological evidence that may be closer to politics than individual characteristics. For example, some scholars argue that communities that tend to be lower-class have more crime which leads to more suspicion that ultimately creates mutual distrust between the police and community. This distrust lends itself nicely to abuse and police involvement.[9]

Another source of possible discretion involves the context of the crime. Those who interact with law enforcement regularly will eventually hear a story about how a suspect "acted" when approached by someone in a police uniform. This is not the entire story of situational variables that can contribute to discretion. Others include the location of the crime, the relationships of the victim and criminal, whether or not witnesses were available, seriousness of the crime, as well as additional criminal characteristics such as race, age, and gender.[10]

---

[8] See Supra note 5.

[9] James Q. Wilson (1968). Varieties of Police Behavior, Harvard University Press: MA. The assertion is that lower class neighborhoods have more crime and that the police are more suspicious of these communities. Rossi, et al, 1974 brings the relationship between the police and community to one of distrust and abuse of discretion.

[10] For some discussions of these individual characteristics, see Ferdinand (1980). Police Attitudes and Police Organization: Some Interdepartmental and Cross Cultural Comparisons Police Studies v 3, pp. 46-60. Ericson (1982). Reproducing Order: A Study of Police Work, University of Toronto Press: Canada. Research in Crime and Delinquency, pp 69-100.

Scholarly attention of discretion has also focused on characteristics of the officer. Some argue that education plays a mixed role in the use of discretion. On one hand, it is argued that more highly educated officers will exercise discretion more often. On the other hand, some scholars have found that college educated officers' experience more negative feelings toward their work.[11] Age and the experience of the officer have also been linked. Older officers tend to believe less in the ideal of police work, while experienced officers use more discretion.

At this point, it is appropriate to speculate as to what accounts for discretion. Those interested in discretion have put forth a number of competing explanations. Therefore, a review of the literature brings us to where we started: What is the role of politics in the use of discretion? Current discretion work evolves around the organizational, situational, and individual aspects of police work at the expense of examining politics. The one thing we know about police officers is that they are savvy and aware of the context in which their work takes place. Politics does indeed account for some use of discretion. While previous research does not use the term politics, it does use the language of politics when describing discretion of police work as it relates to power, wealth, and neighborhood effects.

Some evidence suggests that police officers are immediately aware of where crime occurs and the social station of the victim and perpetrator.[12] Victims and criminals with wealth and power are more likely to be given the benefit

---

[11] L. Sherman (1976) The Effects of College Education on the Maintenance of Police Cynicism, Journal of Police Science and Administration, v 4, pp 340-345.

[12] Smith & Klien see note 10, Westley (1970). Violence and the Police: A Sociological Study of Law, Custom, and Morality, MIT Press: MA and Smith 1986, see note 7.

of the doubt when conflict arises; officers believe they can reason with these individuals, and are less likely to subject individuals of higher socio-economic status to arrest. Some, certainly not all, of these discretionary tendencies are motivated by politics. Anecdotal accounts exist of officers not arresting star athletes, elected officials, and campaign contributors. These examples are not entirely negative aspects of discretion, but they do have some real consequences.

Political considerations and law enforcement discretion is a matter of justice. We know for certain that police officers decide daily when to invoke sanction and when to overlook transgressions. These decisions are explained by a number of motivating factors, one of which can be politics. Political considerations are surrogates for law enforcement's respect of wealth and power, as well as trust and benevolence. As prior research has shown, those with wealth, power, and connections are less likely to be arrested. Their communities are viewed more favorably than those of lower economic position. Trust, cooperation, and support of the police function are greater in communities of enhanced wealth and power. History is replete with the use of law enforcement for political purposes. It stands to reason that some of the discretion of law enforcement, even in an era of heightened professionalism, education, and organizational structure, is still motivated by a respect for class and position that is directly tied to wealth and power.

It may be difficult to directly observe when political considerations influence the work of law enforcement. What we offer is more than conjecture in that the public administrative function has experienced difficulty separating itself from the politics that set its tasks.[13] Law enforcement must be cognizant of the political process and the political

[13] Woodrow Wilson elaborated a dichotomy of politics and administration.

landmines that populate the terrain over which they discharge their duties. By not using the full range of discretionary motivations that guide their work, they run the very great risk of limiting their ability to respond to crime, to detect it, and to solve it. They also could hinder their work through more distrust and lack of cooperation. Law enforcement benefits from maintaining a balanced relationship between itself and society. Political considerations are one small aspect of the balance that law enforcement must maintain as it goes about its daily work.

State Attorneys

State attorneys are in the center of dispensing justice. They serve as a fulcrum in the processing of cases handled by their officers. Just as law enforcement has a dancing act in order to maintain its balance within the justice system, state prosecutors are engaged in more of a juggling act. This juggling of the many and varied parties interested in justice ultimately determines their success or failure and by extension, the quality of justice. The different relationships that must be maintained by prosecutors are displayed in Figure 3-1.

Figure 3-1: Relationships of State Attorneys

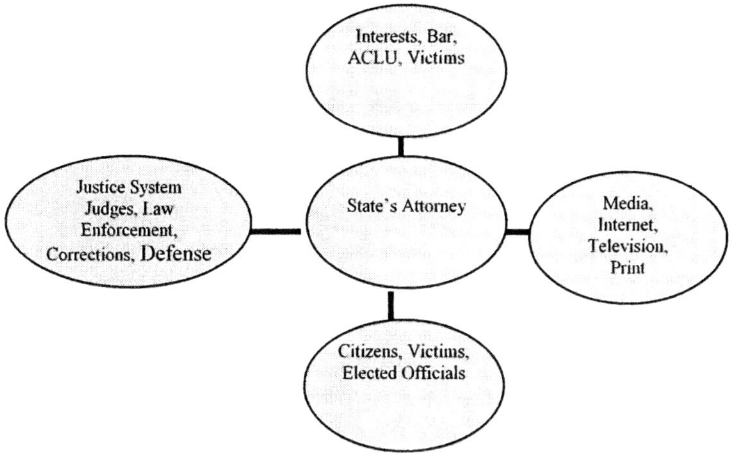

Political Nature of State Attorneys

State attorneys, district attorneys, attorney generals and solicitor generals are by their nature politicians. Most state attorneys are elected or appointed to their posts. The most common method of becoming a state attorney is election which requires a certain amount of politicking. Their assistants and associates are either appointed or staff attorneys. Either way, most state attorneys owe their position to a political process. Once elected, the politics really begins.

As depicted in Figure 3-1, state attorneys deal with a multitude of relationships in order to efficiently and effectively discharge their duties. Victims and their advocacy groups want criminals charged with the maximum charge and promptly, bar associations and other interest groups want the procedural law followed faithfully and for the legal profession to protect all rights of each party to a criminal complaint.

Citizens often desire certain crimes to be taken seriously such as murder, rape, and robbery. Judges don't want frivolous charges and flimsy evidence introduced in their court. Criminal defense attorneys are often perceived to be "sharks" that are without a moral compass. Moreover, within the legal profession their reputation is low. Media outlets have the motto "if it bleeds it leads," while ate the same time devoting many resources to daily trifles of the justice system. The media also serves a spotlight role that uncovers the work of state attorneys, and law enforcement by portraying them either positively or negatively. As such, the media has a strong influence on the discretion of state attorneys.

The many relationships in Figure 3-1 are what George Cole (1970) calls prosecutor clientele.[14] These relationships represent instances where prosecutors must exercise discretion, including political discretion, in order to maintain the effectiveness of his or her office. By neglecting to maintain these relationships, prosecutors run the risk of alienating their office from the rest of the justice system. Law enforcement makes arrests, gathers evidence, and testifies to facts. If their work is continually dismissed due to the decision to not prosecute, then law enforcement becomes disenchanted with their work and ability to achieve justice. Thus, the greatest decision a prosecutor can make is whether to pursue a case or not. This duty is commonly referred to as prosecutorial discretion. We contend that prosecutorial discretion is a political decision.

Prosecutors also need to maintain relationships with their courtroom counterparts and judges. They must make assessments of the options available to judges, in regards to sentencing, and to defense attorneys who may view their role as shepherding cases through the system.[15] Prosecutors also

---

[14] George Cole (1970). Law and Society Review, vol 4, pp. 313-343.
[15] Milton Heimann (1970). Plea Bargaining, University of Chicago Press.

need to be aware of a judge's tendencies when admitting evidence, sentencing, and conduct standards for trial. Thus, prosecutors must gauge what cases are amenable to certain judges, the judge's track record for reducing charges, dismissal, and options for dispensing punishment. Judges and prosecutors are human beings who have limits placed on their discretion by the sheer lack of available options. State attorneys routinely recognize that their role in facilitating the work of law enforcement, defense attorneys, and judges is a political role.[16]

Perhaps the most intriguing relationships prosecutors must manage are what Cole (1970) describes as "community influentials."[17] We broadly construe community influentials to include those who provide the external environment or context within which prosecutors do their work. Community influentials are those individuals or groups that have an interest in the discretion exercised by state attorneys. Within any community there are individuals and institutions that have more power than regular citizens.[18] The media, elected officials and "power elite" each have a vested interest in the exercise of prosecutorial discretion.

Within a democracy, the media acts as a watchdog on the behalf of citizens. It is their responsibility to inform the

---

[16] See Supra note 14.

[17] See Supra note 15.

[18] The community and power studies of scholars such as C. Wright Mills and Floyd Hunter indicate a small group of individuals within any community or society wield "power". That is to say they can "make things happen". Peter Secchia, former ambassador to Italy during the Ford administration, once made the comment that there indeed are people within the community that "make things happen". He was referring to some flack over the costs associated with the City of Grand Rapids, MI providing police protection for his birthday party attended by Vice President Dick Cheney. The overtime costs came at a time when the city was under a hiring freeze and experiencing severe budget shortfalls.

public of official actions by their elected and appointed representatives. As such, the media not only informs but often interprets the actions of elected officials. This "gatekeeper" role of information is powerful politically as public officials know all too well that their decisions are part of a record that can be scrutinized by the public and the media as an agent of the citizenry.[19] Prosecutors don't want to be seen as ignoring a public problem—drugs, corruption, abuse, neglect—or showing too much deference to the elite decision makers within a community.[20]

In addition to the media, various interest groups such as victims' rights groups, bar associations, and those dedicated to protecting the rights of the accused scrutinize the work of prosecutors.[21] Over the past twenty-years, victims' rights advocates have exerted a strong influence to encourage prosecutors to take seriously crimes involving domestic violence, child exploitation, and sexual. Conversely, those who speak for criminals point to the fact that the United State's justice system is predicated upon innocence and have fought to ensure that justice is not tainted by an over reliance on the participation of victims in the prosecution of their own case.[22] The point here is not whether victims should have a

---

[19] Politicians and the media have an important relationship. Almost all decisions made by public officials, particularly those elected officials who work near sophisticated media outlets, are weighed against an objective of how their decisions will be interpreted and perceived by the public. This is a powerful check on behavior and use of power and discretion.

[20] During the era of prohibition, and even in some parts of the United States currently, some justice actors such as Sheriffs and Prosecutors would overlook illegal activities related to gambling, alcohol, and other illegal behaviors.

[21] Paul Robinson (May 6, 2002). "Should the Victims' Rights Movement Have Influence Over Criminal Law Formulation and Adjudication?" University of Pennsylvania Law School. Scholarship at Penn Law.

[22] Aclu.org. This site is maintained by the American Civil Liberties Union. They contend, along with others, that interest group pressures have the

greater role in the work of the justice system, but that interest groups actively seek to influence the work of government any time a decision is made that dispenses a scarce public good such as justice.

Powerful citizens comprise the final relationship depicted in Figure 3-1. These individuals are those who expect preferential treatment from both law enforcement and prosecutors if they run afoul of the law. They also include those on the other side of justice who are not engaged in questionable activities, but seek to maintain order and their power through an equitable enforcement of the laws that ultimately protect their hold on power. As Dye contends, the power elite seek to maintain their governing authority through order maintenance and promoting the values they hold for society. If the work of the justice system disrupts the ability of the elite to govern, they will exert influence over the justice system to remedy a perceived incorrect application of the law or exercise of discretion.[23] For example, a drug ridden community saturated with social ills will petition those "community influentials" to respond to their plight.[24]

Prosecutors have several complex relationships to manage in order to effectively discharge their duties and maintain a hold on power. Perhaps the easiest aspect of the

---

ability to undermine justice. Their work buttresses our argument that interest groups are active and do have some influence on the prosecutorial discretion.

23 Dye contends that the governing elite control information, promote shared values such as property rights, limited government, and minimal regulation of society.

24 This may be manifested in citizen accusations that the police and prosecutors ignore their community or their "part of town." Elite theory, as we developed in Chapter 2, would expect some reaction by the community elite to mollify these concerns so the work of governing can proceed in other areas such as economic development, job creation, and promotion of other "public goods."

prosecutorial role is the actual practicing of law. Regardless, the notion that prosecutorial discretion is not a respecter of both legal and extralegal influences is a flat refusal to acknowledge the myriad relationships that must be massaged in order the maintain the balance of justice. Some have argued, that the juggling act by all members of the justice system is not blind but conducted with extreme acuity as to the tenuous political considerations that must be entertained in order to discharge justice.[25]

Judicial Discretion

Judges have the most discretion of all judicial actors. Of course, law enforcement makes the decision to arrest and prosecutors decide to prosecute. Both exercise a healthy level of discretion. It is judges that are the supreme actor in the courtroom. Recently, the decision of judges has come under scrutiny as the balance of political power is seen to rest with the decisions of judges.[26] Here we will briefly examine a couple of issues related to judicial discretion as more will be treated in chapter four where a full blown discussion of judicial selection, decision-making, and policy making will be covered.

Judges and their behavior are mysterious to most citizens. This is not an indictment of the level of information held by citizens concerning judges, but rather a testament to the power of the myth of judging and the role it plays in maintaining the United States' system of justice. Judges are thought to be wise, fair, honest, and above political

---

[25] See Matthew Robinson (2004). Justice Blind: Ideals and Realities of American Criminal Justice, Prentice Hall: NJ.

[26] While this monograph was being drafted, Justice Sandra Day O'Connor retired. Her decision set off a flurry of activity as the balance of the Supreme Court's power was available through the ability to replace her.

pressures.[27] Normatively, judges should exhibit these qualities and many do. Empirically, we know that judges are as political as sheriffs, police chiefs, prosecutors, and other elected officials. Essentially, judges are politicians who maintain policy preferences and seek to move policy in the direction that is consistent with his or her ideology. Thus, we can view judges in a number of ways: elite politicians, policy makers, and promoters of justice according to their own views of society, human behavior, and governance. Passive observers of judicial behavior in all probability are familiar with the latter role; those of a judge as politician and policy maker may be new. We suspect that the obscurity and mystery of judges and judicial discretion is fading. Their role as policy maker is fully recognized, especially those with an above average interest in politics.

Activism v. Restraint

Judges who view themselves as important players in the realm of policy making are more likely to engage in what is called judicial activism. Rather than strictly adhering to precedent or *stare decisis*, judges seek to make new laws and establish landmark decisions. Within criminal justice, some observers believe that the judiciary has expanded the rights of the accused which hinders justice.[28] Civil rights proponents were elated that *Plessey v. Ferguson* was overturned by *Brown v. Board of Education*.[29] Had precedent been followed, we likely would not have a universal right to an attorney, notification of

---

[27] Edward Lazarus (2004). Life tenure for federal judges: Should it be abolished? FindLaw columnist special to cnn.com.

[28] H. Rothwax (1995). Guilty: The Collapse of Criminal Justice, Random House: NY.

[29] Plessey established the separate but equal doctrine with regard to public accommodations. Brown overturned the decision.

charges, prohibitions against the death penalty in certain cases, a limited right to medical privacy, environmental protections, access to housing and educational opportunities or public employment. Civil liberties have been expanded by activist judges who interpret the Constitution in a way that conveys rights not expressly granted to government. When activist judges use their policy making role in a way inconsistent with either conservative or liberal ideology, political accusations arise and pressure is brought to bear on their deliberations.

Restraint

Some judges view their work as that of an umpire. Rather than change the rules of the game (politics), they judge the actions of citizens, corporations, and governments against an established set of criteria embodied in statues, codes, administrative regulations, and case law. Within a restraint approach, new rights and liberties would be rarely articulated and power would stay vested in executive and legislative officials, as well as bureaucrats. The judiciary would of course judge their actions against the standards already mentioned, but would slowly articulate additional rights and liberties, and even Constitutional protections, through their decisions. Judicial restraint is somewhat limited in that we can see over time an expansion and contraction of the policy scope articulated by judges. Thus, even judges exercising restraint have policy preferences.[30]

---

[30] Lee Epstein & Jack Knight (1997). The Choices Justices Make, CQ Press: Washington, D.C. and Keith Krehbiel (1998). Pivotal Politics: A Theory of U.S. Lawmaking, University of Chicago Press; IL.

Summary

That justice actor's exercise judgment is a fairly straightforward proposition. We contend that one of the primary influences upon their judgment or discretion is politically motivated. If we assume that justice actors are politicians, then we can take some more advanced steps toward understanding their behavior. Political science has been engaged in explaining the behavior of political actors, but students of criminal justice have been hesitant to adopt the methodologies of public administration, economics, and political science for the purpose of understanding justice actors.

The mythologized understanding of the police, prosecutors, and judges serves several purposes: lessens criticism and scrutiny, promote acceptance of decisions, and assure legitimacy. What we know is that the reality of discretionary practices severely undermines the myth of our understanding. Discretion is a necessary element of justice. Without it, justice may be more severely injured than an uneven exercise of discretion. Thus, while discretion has the potential to create miscarriages of justice, it is best understood as something desirable.

To be fair, most of the scholarly literature recognizes politics as inherent in the justice system. This chapter demonstrates explicitly the impact of politics on justice. However, why is politics a desirable part of justice work? We maintain that several issues exist that must be kept in mind when attempting to understand how powerful discretion is and how it relates politics.

Discretion is a matter of using one's best judgment to make a decision. We recognize that poor decisions are made with respect to justice issues. When the best decision is compromised due to politics, a miscarriage of justice occurs.

The remedy for poor decision making is to substitute decision makers. If each decision maker is influenced by the same environment, it is unreasonable to expect better or different decisions. Thus, politics may cause inferior decisions more often and the remedy would be to limit discretion and political influences upon the decisions of justice actors. This will never happen in a legitimate democracy.

Those who bemoan the influence of politics upon the justice process would not trade their ability to influence justice in exchange for a system run by experts or technocrats.[31] That politics and discretion are mutually inclusive of one another is an *a priori* assumption. We don't need experience to know that humans have ideas, act on them, and seek to shape their environment in a way consistent with their beliefs. Thus, eliminating politics rids our system of governance of popular input. Eradicating the system of discretion makes the system more inefficient and further reduces popular control of government. Politicized justice is the price that must be paid for citizen control of the mechanisms of government, including the justice system.

---

[31] Dan Pound (1990). Civic Culture in a Managerial and Technological Society, Kendall-Hunt: Dubuque, IA.

Chapter Four Law Enforcement and Politics

Social control is an issue that often politically polarizes individuals. Throughout civilization, societies have created rules to govern behavior of individuals while assigning punishments for those who break the law. At the center of this dichotomy are the police. For a moment, ask yourself, what is the role of police in our society? What should be the goals of police in the twenty-first century? Do we want police officers who are crime fighters or public servants? This dilemma is ultimately a source of conflict for officers. What are the differences between the two? The crime control officer (conservative ideology) assumes, "criminals are the enemy and fundamentally different from good people. Police are the army that fights the enemy, using any means necessary to control, capture, and punish criminals. Moreover, good people accept and understand that police are in a war and must be allowed deference in their decision making because they–not us- are the experts and only they know the enemy.[1] In contrast, the public servant (liberal ideology) assumes criminals are not a distinct group. These individuals shop, pay taxes, have children and often are our next-door neighbors. Further, public servants serve all people, which include criminals. In effect, there is no enemy, or if there is then the enemy is us.[2] Society's citizens must be cognizant of the fact that police officers legally have the ability to control citizens. This control of citizens has often led to bloodshed.[3] In our

[1] Joycelyn Pollock (2004). Ethics in Crime and Justice. Wadsworth: Belmont, CA.
[2] Id. p.135.
[3] Between the years 1964-1968, riots were breaking out in the United States at a rampant pace. For example, in 1964, a Caucasian officer shot and killed an African-American teenager in New York. African American

democratic society, individuals have the ability to express their beliefs, attitudes, and ideologies. All too often, people will share their opinion on issues such as capital punishment, abortion, birth control, and homosexuality. At the core of this ability to express is the United States Constitution's Bill of Rights.[4] In addition, citizen's behavior is surrounded by

---

leaders in Harlem led a protest demanding disciplinary action against the officer. After several days of turmoil, the protestors began throwing rocks at the precinct headquarters. Two days later, burning and looting were accompanied by one death, 100 injured, 500 arrested and millions of dollars of damage. In 1965, Los Angeles (Watt's riot) thirty-four persons died, over one thousand were injured and four-thousand were arrested. By 1966, over 43 riots erupted. In 1967, Newark, New Jersey and Detroit, Michigan riots resulted in 67 deaths and millions in property damage.

[4] The Bill of Rights (1791) refers to the first ten amendments of the United States Constitution. Amendments I, IV, V, VI and VIII pertain to the daily functioning of the Criminal Justice system. Amendment I: Congress shall make no law respecting an establishment of religion, or prohibiting the free exercise thereof; or abridging the freedom of speech, or the process; or the right of the people peaceably to assemble, and to petition the Government for a redress of grievances. Amendment IV: The right of the people to be secure in their persons, houses, papers, and affects, against unreasonable searches and seizures, shall not be violated, and no warrants shall issue, but upon probable cause, supported by oath or affirmation, and particularly describing the place to be searched, and the persons or things to be seized. Amendment V: No person shall be held to answer for a capital, or otherwise infamous crime, unless on a presentment or indictment of a Grand Jury, except in cases arising in the land or naval forces, or in the Militia, when in actual service in time or War or public danger; nor shall any person be subject for the same offence to be twice put in jeopardy of life or limb; nor shall be compelled in any criminal case to be a witness against himself, nor be deprived of life, liberty, or property taken for public use, without just compensation. Amendment VI: In all criminal prosecutions, the accused shall enjoy the right to a speedy and public trial, by an impartial jury of the State and district wherein the crime shall have been committed, which district shall have been previously ascertained by law, and to be informed of the nature and cause of the accusation; to be confronted with the witnesses against him; to have compulsory process for

perimeters that guide everyday behavior. For example, citizens are guided by the state constitutions, state statutes and city ordinances. When an individual crosses beyond the boundaries of these perimeters, then society often deems this behavior as unacceptable. The behavior may range from public drunkenness, which is a city ordinance, to murder, which could be a federal and state crime.[5] Interestingly, another perimeter that is prevalent in our daily lives is the social contract.[6] This hypothetical contract is a voluntary agreement among individuals which defines the relationship of individuals with one another and government. Through this process, an organized society is formed. Does everyone follow and adhere to the unwritten contract? Of course the answer is no! Why might individuals cross the threshold of acceptable and engage in unacceptable behavior? Could the answer be poverty, racial bias and discrimination, a lack of legitimate opportunities or the perception of unequal justice? In reality, there exist citizens who feel marginalized and frustrated with their life as well as the status quo. Citizens may experience

---

obtaining witnesses in his favor, and to have the Assistance of Counsel for his defense. Amendment VIII: Excessive bail shall not be required, nor excessive fines imposed, nor cruel and unusual punishments inflicted.

[5] Murder is considered a common law crime. Murder is often refereed to as a "mala in se" crime (inherently evil in and of itself). Common law has no statutory basis. Judges develop common law through their written opinions, which are binding on future decisions of lower courts in the same jurisdiction. Important, common law is a fluid dynamic which evolves or changes over time. Individual states have their own common laws on many topics.

[6] See Thomas Hobbes, John Locke and John Rawls. Social Contract in essence is a contract (in theory) or an agreement whereas individuals accept certain restrictions on them for the benefit of society. The restrictions are often enforced by the government and usually take the shape of laws.

helplessness[7] or succumb to a self fulfilling prophecy.[8] Citizens may indulge in drugs or alcohol as an escape mechanism. Citizens may contemplate suicide,[9] question their religious beliefs or even harm others. Figure 4-1 demonstrates how these individual thoughts, beliefs and behaviors exist among the established perimeters.

Figure 4-1: Societal Fluid Chaos Model

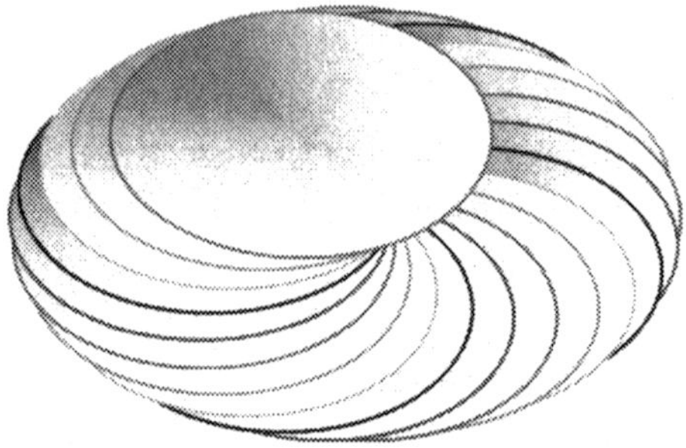

While law enforcement is an important element of the societal fluid chaos model, the success of the various departments (order maintenance and deviance control and crime rate and recidivism) is never congruent with society as a whole. To illustrate, local, as well as national news programs such as CNN, Fox News, MSNBC, CNBC and Court TV, often televise stories of law enforcement officers exhibiting

---

[7] Martin Seligman (1975). conducted a series of experiments which resulted in the psychological concept of learned helplessness.
[8] Robert Merton (1948). Self Fulfilling Prophecy.
[9] Emile Durkheim (1897). Suicide: A Study in Sociology (1951). Translated by John Spaulding and George Simpson. The Free Press of Glenco: NY:NY.

unacceptable conduct. Whether good or bad, law enforcement officers are the most visible component of the criminal justice system. The focus of this chapter is to examine contemporary issues which often prohibit law enforcement officers from performing their duties effectively. Moreover, these issues are consequently those which are the most politicized. These issues include socialization, excessive force, police corruption and racial profiling.

Socialization

Socialization is a process that occurs over time. In essence, socialization is the dynamic process of learning a culture.[10] On a macro level, individuals are socialized into a specific culture. As for the micro level, we must recognize that socialization occurs in police departments throughout the United States. Important to recognize is the fact that, "police are selected based on demonstrated conformity to dominant social norms and values. Those who become police officers bring to the occupation the perceptual baggage and moral standards common to the working middle class."[11] With the passage of time, officers learn via socialization what is acceptable and unacceptable behavior. This behavior is often referred to as the police subculture. The police subculture is defined as "the values and perceptions that are shared by members of a police department and to a certain extent, by all law enforcement agents. These values and perceptions are shared by the unique and isolated existence of the police officer."[12] Examples of

---

[10] Socialization is discussed extensively in sociological literature.
[11] Victor Kappeler, Richard Sluder & Geoffrey Alpert (1998). Forces of Deviance: The Dark Side of Policing. 2nd edition. Waveland Press, Prospect Heights, IL.
[12] Larry Gaines & Roger Leroy Miller (2006). Criminal Justice in Action: The Core. Thomson Wadsworth: Belmont, CA.

values or perceptions within the subculture are isolation, secrecy, autonomy, solidarity, autonomy, bravery, loyalty and cynicism.[13] Ultimately, these values and perceptions foster an "us versus them mentality." In return, law enforcement officers view citizens as outsiders who should be viewed with caution. To best illustrate how these values and perceptions are manifested in the lives of law enforcement officers is through the use of postulates. Postulates "are the verbal links between a subculture's view of the world and the translation of that view into action."[14] According to Reuss-Ianni (1983), law enforcement officers are expected to:

- Watch out for their partner first and then the rest of the guys working that tour.
- Don't give up another cop.
- Show balls.
- Be aggressive when you have to, but don't be too eager.

---

[13] There is a great deal of discussion pertaining to subculture values, perceptions and themes. See Van Maanen (1978). "The Asshole" in P. Manning & J. Van Maanen, Policing: A View from the Streets, pp.221-240. Goodyear Publishing Company, Santa Monica, CA, Lawrence Sherman (1982), "Learning Police Ethics" Criminal Justice Ethics, 1(1), pp.10-19, Joycelyn Pollock (2004). Ethics in Crime and Justice. Thomson/Wadsworth: Belmont, CA. Victor Kappeler, Richard Sluder & Geoffrey Alpert (1998). Breeding Deviant Conformity: The Ideology and Culture of Police, In Roger Dunham and Geoffrey Alpert (2005). Critical Issues in Policing: Contemporary Readings, Waveland Press, Long Grove, IL. Peter Manning The Police: Mandate, strategies and appearances. In V.E. Kappler (ED) The Police & Society: Touchstone Readings. Prospect Heights, IL, Waveland Press, E. Reuss Ianni (1983). Two Cultures of Policing. New Brunswick, NJ: Transaction Books.

[14] Victor Kappeler, Richard Sluder & Geoffrey Alpert (1998). Breeding Deviant Conformity: The Ideology and Culture of Police. In Roger Dunham & Geoffrey Alpert (2005). Critical Issues in Policing: Contemporary Readings. Waveland Press, Long Grove, IL.

- Don't get involved in anything in another guy's sector.
- Hold up your end of the work.
- If you get caught off base, don't implicate anybody else.
- Make sure the other guy knows if another cop is dangerous or crazy.
- Don't trust a new guy until you have checked him out.
- Don't tell anybody else more than they have to know; it could be bad for you and it could be bad for them.
- Don't talk too much or too little.
- Protect your ass.
- Don't make waves.
- Don't look for favors just for yourself.[15]

When examining the socialization of law enforcement in the context of the societal fluid chaos model, one can understand why citizens are frustrated and have little confidence in their local police departments. Citizenry expect law enforcement officers to uphold the United States and State Constitutions, federal and state laws, and city ordnances. Interestingly, law enforcement departments begin the selection process with a preconceived notion as to which rookie cops fit into a certain mold, subject these individuals to a 12-16 week academy where instructors (former street cops) tell war stories of the old days. Moreover, at the academy, the curriculum is asymmetric (practical not intellectually challenging). Upon graduation, these new recruits are assigned a FTO who was hand picked by the departments administration. The FTO is to acquaint the rookie with the ins and outs or the dos and don'ts of the department (socialization and subculture). Ultimately,

---

[15] E Reuss-Ianni. (1983). Two Cultures of Policing: Street Cops and Management Cops. New Brunswick, NJ. Transaction Books.

the officer learns the postulates or informal code. As the days, months and years pass by; you have an officer who hides behind a blue curtain of secrecy. This officer may have witnessed on many occasions an injustice however, due to socialization. i.e. subculture, the officer is scared to come forward.

Excessive Force

In New York City in (1999), four police officers were searching for a rape suspect. The officers going door to door came across Amadou Diallo. As police were attempting to speak with him he reached inside his jacket. In a matter of seconds, officers shot at Diallo forty one times while successfully striking him nineteen times. The immigrant was attempting to obtain his wallet. On March 2, 1991, Rodney King spent the night watching basketball and drinking heavily. Later that evening while driving home, King passed a police vehicle and subsequently led police on a high speed chase. Eventually, twelve police cars, a helicopter, and twenty-seven officers were involved in apprehending King. As a result, King suffered eleven skull fractures, a broken cheekbone, a fractured eye socket, a broken ankle, internal and external bruises, missing teeth, brain damage and kidney damage.[17] While the above examples demonstrate aggravated forms of deadly and excessive force, society must understand that the daily life of a law enforcement officer brings a multitude of challenges. In one instance, an officer may be performing an

---

[17] Victor Kappeler, Richard Sluder & Geoffrey Alpert (1994). Forces of Deviance: Understanding the Dark Side of Policing. Waveland Press: Prospect Heights,IL.

order maintenance function, while thirty minutes later, deviance control. In either situation, the law enforcement officer has the ability to control citizens. Control is manifested through four elements: power, authority, persuasion, and force.[18] Power is often symbolized via a firearm, baton or handcuffs. Authority can be understood as an ability to command with the expectation of being obeyed. Persuasion is often used before the use of force is employed, however, persuasion does not have to be followed by those with power.[19] Force can be defined as, "the use of physical restraint by a police officer when dealing with a member of the public." Whereas, excessive force is, "the application of an amount and or frequency of force greater than that required to compel compliance from a willing or unwilling suspect."[20] Regrettably, "the authority to use force in the line of duty is one of the most controversial aspects of police work. While it is a necessary tool for officers in controlling crime and apprehending criminals, it also is the greatest source of police abuse of authority and citizen complaints. Police officers have the right to use force in certain specific situations, but questions are raised as to when it should be employed and how much force is necessary."[21] As the above examples demonstrate, there are two types of force: non-deadly and deadly. Examples of non-deadly force include the use of pepper spray, pistols that fire beanbags or rubber bullets, stun guns or tear gas. Important to recognize is that, the use of non-deadly force is, "regulated by the concept of reasonable force,

---

[18] Carl Klockars (1984). Blue Lies and Police Placebos. American Behavioral Scientist, 27 (4): pp.529-544.
[19] See Supra note 1.
[20] International Association of Chiefs of Police (2001). Police Use of Force in America 2001. p. 1 Alexandra, VA.
[21] Roger Dunham & Geoffrey Alpert (2005). Critical Issues in Policing: Contemporary Readings. p.433. Waveland Press: Long Grove: IL.

which allows the use of non-deadly force when a reasonable person would assume that such force was necessary. In contrast, deadly force is force that an objective police officer realizes will place the subject in direct threat of serious injury or death."[22] How prevalent is deadly force in the United States? According to the Department of Justice (2001), there were 8,578 justifiable homicides from 1976-1998. On average, 373 felons are lawfully killed by police each year.[23] By comparison, of the estimated 45.3 million U.S. residents who had at least one face to face contact with a police officer in (1999), 664,500 stated that the police used or threatened force against them.[24] In addition, 75% characterized the force as excessive, 87% believed the police acted improper, and African Americans and Hispanics are more likely than Caucasians to be threatened or experience the use of force during the contact.[25]

Law Enforcement Corruption

Law Enforcement officers and corruption has been an issue since the birth of Policing. As discussed previously, officers are bestowed with the ability to control via the use of power, authority, persuasion and force. Not surprisingly, there exist some law enforcement officers who will take advantage of the

---

[22] Larry Gaines & Roger Leroy Miller (2006). Criminal Justice in Action: The Core. p.148. Thomson: Wadsworth: Belmont; CA.
[23] Jodi Brown & Patrick Langan (2001). Policing and Homicide, 1976-98: Justifiable Homicide by Police, Police Officers Murdered by Felons. U.S. Department of Justice: Bureau of Justice Statistics.
[24] Patrick Langan, Matthew Durose &Erica Schmitt (2002). Contacts between Police and the Public. U.S. Department of Justice: Bureau of Justice Statistics. See *Tennessee v. Garner* (1985) and *Graham v. Connor* (1989) for a case analysis of the use of reasonable and deadly force.
[25] Id.

public's trust and confidence for their own gain. In addition, some police departments have a constant history of corruption. For example, "wide-scale investigations occurred in 1894, 1913, 1932 (the Wickersham commission), 1949 (the Kefauver Commission), 1972 (the Knapp Commission), and 1993 (the Mollen Commission)."[26] Why some law enforcement officers participate in corruption is not difficult to understand when considering that the relationship between police and citizens is asymmetric. Moreover, the nature of policing is abundant with opportunities to engage in illegal activities. For example, policing is characterized by discretion and activities that occur in private settings with an absence of supervisors.[27] The consequences of corruption often affect the officer and department for years. Officers engaged in corruption may be terminated and ultimately face the possibility of a civil suit(s) and/or criminal charges. Moreover, the department's integrity is questioned. When corruption occurs, the community and law enforcement officers throughout the nation are harmed by the behavior of officers. With this discussion of corruption, how should we define it? While corruption manifests itself in many ways, the common denominator is the extent to which law enforcement officers use their authority for personal gain. Corruption is also subjective and open for debate. According to Schmalleger (2005) corruption ranges from:

Gratuities: accepting small favors such as free coffee and meals.

---

[26] S. Rothlein (1999). Policy Agency Efforts to Prevent Abuses. In G. Lynch (ed) Human Dignity and the Police: Ethics and Integrity in Police Work, pp.15-27. . Charles C. Thomas: Springfield, IL.

[27] Carl Klockars (2000). The Measurement of Police Integrity. National Institute of Justice Research Brief. Washington DC.

Playing Favorites: not administering a ticket to a friend who was speeding (selective enforcement).

Minor Bribes: accepting minor sums of money in return for favors, such as looking the other way on a ticket.

Being above Inconvenient Laws: not enforcing such laws as speeding, smoking marijuana, and drinking.

Role Malfeasance: Destruction of evidence, biased testimony, protection of crooked cops.

Major Bribes: accepting large sums of money in return for overlooking law violations.

Property Crimes: committing acts such as burglary or theft

Criminal Enterprise: the resale of confiscated property or drugs.

Denial of Civil Rights: routine schemes to circumvent constitutional guarantees of due process (planting evidence).

Violent Crimes: physical abuse of suspects, including torture and non-justifiable homicide.[28]

As the above demonstrates, corruption exists on a continuum that ranges from gratuities to violent crimes. Obviously, depriving a citizen of due process is illegal; however, does the acceptance of a free meal constitute

---

[28] Frank Schmalleger (2005). Criminal Justice Today: An Introductory Text for the 21st Century. P.330. Pearson: Prentice Hall. Upper Saddle River, NJ.

corruption? What about an officer who receives free dry cleaning or liquor? Is it possible that receiving small gratuities will eventually lead to the acceptance of minor bribes or the commission of violent crimes? Those who answer in the affirmative, hold the perspective of the slippery slope.[29] In contrast, Kania (1988) suggests that the acceptance of minor gratuities by law enforcement officers fosters and builds positive relationships with the public.[30] At the core of the gratuities issue is reciprocity, expectation and obligation. For example, a local chief of police eats for free at a local restaurant establishment for years. One evening the owner of the restaurant is drinking and driving and subsequently is arrested. Is the chief expected or obligated to assist the restaurant owner? To crystallize the issue, let's examine public opinion. According to Jones' (1999), study of North Carolina residents, "one of the pitfalls of police officer gratuities is the creation of public resentment toward law enforcement officials, particularly from segments of the public that have often clashed with police in the past."[31]

Racial Profiling and Biased Policing

Out of desperation, a young Black woman trades her new sports car in for an older model; cops repeatedly stopped her because they suspected she stole it.

A prominent Black lawyer driving a luxury car is stopped

---

[29] Tim Prenzler & Peta Mackay (1995). Police Gratuities: What the Public Thinks. Criminal Justice Ethics. Winter/Spring, pp.15-25.
[30] R. Kania (1988). Police Acceptance of Gratuities. Criminal Justice Ethics, 7(2), pp.37-49.
[31] Mark Jones (1999). Religion, Race and Public Opinion About Police Officer Gratuities. Journal of Contemporary Criminal Justice, Vol. 15, No.2, pp.191-204.

repeatedly on various pretexts.

A Hispanic deputy police chief is stopped numerous times "on suspicion" when he is outside his jurisdiction.

Officers stop a Black judge away from her jurisdiction, handcuff her, and lay her face down on the pavement while they search her car. They find nothing and let her go without a citation.[32]

The above stories (DWB: Driving while Black or Brown) are routinely discussed on our local and national news programs as well as in newspapers across the country. Law enforcement officers throughout the nation are responsible for the equitable treatment of all citizens. The fact that some officers will engage in racial or biased policing should not be surprising. Racial biases that existed in the nineteenth and twentieth century is still prevalent today. With regard to law enforcement, as a whole, the profession is Caucasian and male dominated. As of (2000), racial and ethnic minorities comprised 22.7% of full time sworn personnel; whereas, females comprised 10.6% of officers.[33] Racial profiling "occurs when a police action is initiated by race, ethnicity, or national origin of the suspect, rather than by any evidence or information that the suspect has broken the law."[34] A criticism of this definition is its exclusive focus on race. Reasoning follows that a law enforcement officer who is racially prejudiced will use race and other factors when conducting biased law enforcement. For example, "officers might make

---

[32] Lorie Fridell, Robert Lunney, Drew Diamond, Bruce Kuba, Michael Scott & Colleen Laing (2001). Racially Biased Policing: A Principled Response: Police Executive Research Forum.

[33] Brian Reeves (2000). Local Police Departments. Bureau of Justice Statistics. U.S. Department of Justice.

[34] See Supra note 24 at p. 183.

biased decisions based on the neighborhood and the race of the person, the age of the car and the race of the person, or the gender and the race of the person. Activities based on these sample pairs of factors would fall outside the most commonly used definition of racial profiling."[35] In an effort to broaden the definition, the Police Executive Research Forum in (2001) created the term racially biased policing. According to Fridell (2001), "racial biased policing occurs when law enforcement inappropriately considers race or ethnicity in deciding with whom and how to intervene in an enforcement capacity."[36] At the core of either definition is the issue of race and biases. How prevalent is racially profiling/biased law enforcement officers? According to, "recent national surveys, the majority of white, as well as Black, Americans say that racial profiling is widespread in the United States today."[37] A New Jersey Attorney General report in (1999) reached the conclusion that law enforcement officers had engaged in racial profiling of drivers.[38] Specifically, "people of color constituted 40.6% of the stops made on the turnpike. Although few stops resulted in a search, 77.2% of the individuals searched were people of color."[39] A study in Maryland revealed that African Americans accounted for 17.5% of those violating traffic laws; however, the number of motorists actually stopped and

---

[35] Lorie Fridell & Michael Scott (2005). Law Enforcement Agency Responses to Racially Biased Policing and the Perceptions of Its Practice. pp. 304-321. In Roger Dunham & Geoffrey Alpert (2005). Critical Issues in Policing. Waveland Press: Long Grove, IL.
[36] See Supra note 32.
[37] Id. p. 3.
[38] Peter Verniero & Paul Zoubek (1999). New Jerseys Attorney General's Interim Report of The State Police Review Team Regarding Allegations Of Racial Profiling. Trenton, New Jersey.
[39] See Supra note 28. Deborah Ramirez, Jack McDevitt and Amy Farrell (2000). A Resource Guide on Racial Profiling Data Collection Systems: Promising Practices and Lessons learned. Washington, DC.

searched was 72.9%.[40] Further evidence in Volusa County, Florida suggests that, "70% of the stops and 80% of all searches after stops were directed toward African Americans or Latino, though these groups made up only 5 percent of the drivers."[41] Law enforcement departments throughout the nation should recognize that the American public does not condone this practice. A recent National poll (2003) revealed that 85% of African Americans and 54% of Caucasians believe racial profiling is widespread.[42] Society must recognize that racial profiling/biased policing amongst law enforcement officers weakens and destroys public confidence in the police. A prediction by Ramirez, McDevitt, and Farrell (2000) holds that, "truly effective policing will only be achieved when police both protect their neighborhoods from crime and respect the civil liberties of all residents. When law enforcement practices are perceived to be biased, unfair, or disrespectful, communities of color are less willing to trust and confide in police officers, report crimes, participate in problem-solving activities, be witnesses at trials, or serve on juries."[43]

---

[40] Michael Buerger & Amy Farrell (2002). The Evidence of Racial Profiling: Interpreting Documented and Unofficial Sources. Police Quarterly, Vol. 5 No.3, pp.272-305. Tracy Maclin (1998). Race and the Fourth Amendment, Vanderbilt Law Review.

[41] See Supra note 1 and J. Crank (2003). Imagining Justice. Cincinnati Ohio. Anderson.

[42] Gallup Organization. (2003). Americans See Racial Profiling as Widespread. Washington, DC.

[43] Deborah Ramerez, Jack McDevitt & Amy Farrell (2000). A Resource Guide on Racial Profiling Data Collection Systems: Promising Practices and Lessons Learned, p.3. Bureau of Justice Statistics: U.S. Department of Justice. Washington, DC.

Summary

The United States relies on law enforcement officers to maintain peace (order maintenance and deviance control). Society expects police officers to detect and apprehend those who engage in unacceptable behavior. Perimeters such as the United States and state Constitutions, federal and state statutes, and city ordinances are established as guidelines for everyday behavior. When these guidelines or perimeters are crossed, negative consequences are likely for the violators. Ultimately, how can we (society) have confidence and faith in law enforcement officers when they are engage in unacceptable (lawbreaking) behavior? When citizens view their local and national news outlets depicting acts of excessive force, corruption and racial profiling/biased policing, they have a right to be cynical, critical, and doubtful.

Chapter Five Judicial Politics

Citizens enjoy rights and liberties articulated over time by decisions of judges. Prevailing case law establishes legal guideposts and become common law (judge made law) and a body of procedural law. In the United States, there are laws that outline suitable behavior (statutory law, administrative regulations, codes), and a set of laws that govern how offenders will be treated through the judicial process. Suffice to say that the politics of the judicial process is worth examining in detail given the importance of judges. Thus, this chapter focuses on the politics of the judiciary by taking up three main topics: how judges gain their positions, the influences on their decisions, and their policy making role.

Judicial Ideal

Ideally, judges should be free from political considerations. Federal judges are appointed to life terms pending acceptable behavior.[1] State judges usually take their posts after perhaps distinguished legal careers. Whenever a judicial vacancy occurs, candidates for a judgeship tout their education credentials, victories and defeats, opinions, and legal writings. Those who appoint judges usually remark that they have no litmus test for judges other than competence, qualification, and fitness to judge.[2] Judges who must secure their seat on the bench by running under party label typically make efforts to publicly seem moderate and fair. Thus, the judicial ideal

---

[1] Article III of the U.S. Constitution established the Supreme Court. The Judiciary Act of 1789 established the framework for all courts inferior to the Supreme Court. Almost all state courts are structured similarly to the federal courts i.e. hierarchical with a court of last resort (Supreme Court).

[2] These appear as litmus tests.

would seem to suggest that the judicial branch of government, covering both criminal and civil justice systems, is the most insular from politics.

The judicial ideal that politics would be less of a hindrance to the judicial process was articulated at the founding of the United States by Alexander Hamilton when he wrote "whoever attentively considers the different departments of power must perceive, that, in a government in which they are separated from each other, the judiciary, from the nature of its functions, will always be the least dangerous to the political rights of the Constitution; because it will be least in a capacity to annoy or injure them."[3] Many observers of the court in the United States today (2005) would beg to differ with Mr. Hamilton. It is the courts that ultimately settle all political questions.[4] Since John Marshall claimed the right of the judiciary is to review actions by the other branches of government, the judicial branch (justice branch) has become formidable as an arbiter of justice, potential oppressor of freedom, and policy making branch of government.[5]

Judicial Selection

Judges gain their positions in several ways. At the federal level, judges are appointed by the president, and confirmed by the Senate. States seat judges slightly differently either by appointment, election (popular and legislative), or by a

---

[3] Alexander Hamilton, Federalist Paper #78.

[4] Woodrow Wilson (1916). Speech to the National American Woman Suffrage Association Convention.

[5] *Marbury v. Madison* (1803) established judicial review. The decision was both a legal coup de grace, and a stroke of political genius. Not only Justice Marshall pacify President Jefferson's anti-federalist ideology, he claimed for the judiciary the right to review legislative and executive actions.

combination of appointment and popular election.[6] The different methods of judicial selection seem rather benign. We are very familiar with the notion of executive appointments and popular elections. Therefore, on the surface, no harm seems imminent from electing judges or appointing them. In fact, there may be no discernable difference in the quality of judges, the amount of politics that permeates their work, or what decisions are made with regards to cases and the law. Nevertheless, differences do exist from state to state, as well as federal and state, in the way judges are seated. Those differences are worth scrutinizing for the sake of justice. Normative disruptions caused by varying methods are also fair game for analysis.

Federal Appointments

Since federal judges serve life appointments pending good behavior, their selections have come under increased scrutiny and attention of ideologues, interest groups, and active citizenry. U.S. Supreme Court nominations are fierce political battles because Supreme Court justices wield real and political power.[7] Thus, it is their ability to change policy, overturn laws, and affect the fortunes of millions coupled with the insular nature of the federal judiciary that gives them credence within the United States' political system. To place a finer point on the politics of judicial selection, we need to be aware that the contemporary struggles over the judiciary are mostly attributable to ideology and shifting power that influences

---

[6] The system whereby a judge is appointed is also known as a merit system or the Missouri Plan.

[7] Charles Schumer, July 10, 2005, This Week with George Stephanopoulos asserted that justices are extremely powerful.

decisions of the judiciary. We contend that all political battles associated with the judiciary are fought over ideology.[8]

Sheldon Goldman nicely illustrates that both ideology and partisanship have influenced the selection of federal judges in ways that are intended to achieve policy goals.[9] Goldman's conceptual assumption is that executives have agendas, policy and personal, that can be enhanced through the "right" judicial appointments. Of course, not all executives choose judges based on policy agenda, but all executives choose judges based on political considerations. Ideology, or policy preferences, is the most significant motivating factor.

While the politics of lower court selection may be muted, it is indeed symbolic of the political struggle over the judiciary.[10] No where else do we see the overt politics of judicial selection than appointments to the Supreme Court of the United States. Presidents have realized that the surest way to extend their legacy and influence upon government is through the appointment of a successful Supreme Court nomination.[11] Since the Supreme Court has become somewhat

---

[8] Typically "extreme" ideology at the federal level and partisanship at the state level provides the fuel for most judicial appointment scrapes.

[9] Sheldon Goldman (1997). Picking Federal Judges: Lower Court Selection from Roosevelt through Reagan. His reference to the "lower court" includes all federal courts organizationally below the Supreme Court. His treatment of lower courts is the most thorough, and one of the few scholarly works to devote initial attention to inferior court appointments.

[10] Kermit Hall (1979). The Politics of Justice: Lower Federal Judicial Selection and the Second Party System 1829-1861.

[11] U.S. Presidents have averaged two nominees per term. As citied in J.A. Maltese (1995). The Selling of Supreme Court Nominees, Johns Hopkins University Press: MD. Both Maltese and Goodman reference notes to President Nixon that references the ability to extend presidential power via court nominations.

of a final arbiter on almost all political issues, the tussle over Supreme Court nominees is intense.[12]

Most nominees to the federal bench, including the Supreme Court, are confirmed. Historically, over 80% of Supreme Court nominees have been confirmed.[13] This rate is the lowest success rate for appointed positions, and variations of the confirmation rate mirror the relative equilibrium apparent in the political system.[14] Successful nominations are not accidental. They require careful scrutiny by the President in order to find an acceptable nominee. Justices recently confirmed and rejected by the Senate illustrate nicely some of the political issues surrounding appointed judges.

Robert Bork's rejection as a nominee to the Supreme Court has come to serve as a "shock" to the political system as it relates to judicial nominees.[15] His rejection as a Supreme Court justice serves as a barometer, whereby all future nominees would have a full examination of their politics, ideology, affiliation, culminating in a full fledged campaign waged both for and against their nomination. When these campaigns are successful in sinking a nominee, that person is

---

[12] Nominating a Supreme Court justice has been characterized as a "process" that requires a certain amount of "selling" of the nominee to the Senate, interest groups, and citizenry.

[13] See Supra note 11.

[14] See Supra note 9. References the "flux" of the political system. Maltese at Supra note 11 finds a higher rate of rejection of Supreme Court during the rocky political period beginning in 1968. He contends the level of contention over nominees has to do with the recognition of how important the Court is in settling political issues.

[15] Many texts treat the politics of the Bork nomination including Michael Pertschuk & Wendy Schaetzel, (1989). The People Rising: The Campaign Against the Bork Nomination, Thunder Mouth Press: NY. Ethan Bronner (1989). The Battle for Justice: How the Bork Nomination Shook American, Norton: NY, and Patrick McGuigan and Dawn Weyrich, (1990). Ninth Justice: The Fight for Bork, University Press of America: Washington, DC.

said to have been "borked."[16] Robert Bork was rejected for very straightforward political reasons such as partisanship and ideology. Nominated by Republican President Ronald Reagan, Bork faced a Senate controlled by Democrats. As an appellate judge, Bork had made decisions and articulated beliefs that almost all Democrats and some Republicans found antithetical to civil rights progress.[17] His animosity toward the confirmation process, and an insurmountable obstacle of ideological conflicts ultimately made his confirmation impossible. Disagreement still exists over whether the denied confirmation was a smear or the system of advice and consent working the way it should.[18]

Shortly after Bork's ill fated turn with the Senate, current justice Clarence Thomas experienced his own humiliation at the hands of the nomination and confirmation process. As President Bush's nominee to replace Thurgood Marshall, Thomas' minority status did bring the issue of race at the forefront of characteristics considered in the selection process.[19] However, he faced strong opposition to his nomination based on his ideology and professional conduct while a political appointee. The overriding issue facing Thomas became his leadership of the Equal Employment Opportunity Commission. Anita Hill, a lawyer with the EEOC, accused Thomas of sexual harassment. This accusation

---

[16] Maltese defines being "borked" as an unleashing of "lobbying and public relations of the kind employed successfully against Robert Bork."

[17] Ted Kennedy made an impassioned speech that predicted back alley abortions, denied access to fair employment and higher education, and rogue law enforcement if Bork were on the bench. Arlen Specter, R-Pennsylvania also expressed similar misgivings.

[18] Liberals believe the denying of Bork was a positive. Conservatives viewed his denial as further attacks on responsible governance.

[19] Other than ideology and partisanship, selection characteristics routinely do include a nominee's gender, race, religion, region, credentials, ethnicity, standing in the legal community, competence, integrity, temperament, etc.

was electrified as the Supreme Court, only a few years earlier, had articulated in *Meritor v. Vinson* (1986), that sexual harassment was a civil rights violation. In addition, the EEOC is the federal agency responsible for rooting out discrimination in the workplace. If the Director of the EEOC engaged in violating the civil rights of a staff attorney under his leadership, could he uphold and enforce the civil rights of plaintiffs before the court? Ultimately, Anita Hill seemed implausible and did not significantly sway the Senate. Thomas achieved confirmation even though most Democrats voted against his nomination.[20]

Appointing judges seems like a simple political process; however, it is wrought with considerations that require a sophisticated understanding of politics. Presidents choose nominees for any number of reasons, but most often the motivation is based on how closely agreeable the nominee is to the President's own ideology. In the next section we will discuss judicial decision making, which should illuminate more clearly the contentious nature of executive appointments of judges. Our attention now turns to judicial selection in the states.

State Judicial Selection

Judicial selection in the states is best viewed as a process of evolving methodologies whose aim is to seat the most qualified judge and remove political influences.[21] Currently, most states attempt to select judges based on a modified executive appointment system with many employing commissions that recommend suitable candidates for

---

[20] Thomas was confirmed by a 52-48 vote.

[21] Hajs.org/js/berkon. Larry Berkson and Rachel Caufield. Judicial Selection in the United States: A Special Report.

appointment.[22] Other methods include partisan election, legislative election, and appointment and election. The number of different methods is as numerous as the number of states. Selection methods are varied due to the distinct political history of each state.

Judges who are elected in partisan elections are perhaps the most influenced by politics. By declaring party allegiance, candidates for the bench usually pledge to uphold party positions on policy issues. Political parties exist to organize individuals around a broad set of issues and to elect candidates that generally agree with those positions. It seems contrary to normative expectations of objectivity to otherwise show prejudice on legal matters by affiliating with a political party. In addition, partisan elections require monetary donations that could be seen as "buying" justice. Historically, states have vacillated between appointment and election, and have found both systems lacking. The ultimate question then becomes what difference does the method of selection make?[23]

Most states practice a modified version of the Missouri method of selecting judges. Under the Missouri Plan, judges are selected by a panel to serve for a period of a year and then are subjected to election. Other states have established commissions for original courts and some for appellate courts. The goal is to limit the political rancor associated with judicial selection. Is it safe to assume that politics can be squeezed out of the judicial selection process at the state level? An examination of the Missouri method found many nuances and subtle politics, both of which exist in other methods. Thus,

---

[22] See Supra note 21.

[23] Philip Dubois (1980). From Ballot to Bench: Judicial Election and the Quest for Judicial Accountability, University of Texas Press: TX. Elliot Slotnic (1984). Judicial Selection Systems and Nomination Outcomes: Does the Process Make a Difference, American Politics Quarterly, v. 12, pp. 225-40.

appointment and confirmation do not wring out the politics but shifts the locus of where it originated. Elite preferences will usually prevail in politics. Analysis of less political methods of judicial selection indicates it is just a matter of whose preferences will prevail.[24]

Politics pervades judicial selection at the federal and state levels even though each level of government pursues varying methods of judicial selection. Reformers have argued that it is desirable in a normative sense to remove, as best can be accomplished, politics as a matter of consideration when choosing judges. If politics clouds the process and influences the choice of a judge, justice could be undermined. Observers contend that the judiciary, with a system of checks and balances, was never supposed to be just another policy making body. The judiciary, with judges and the law at the center, was to be free from politics and discharge their duties without regard to popular opinion, concerns for ideological pursuits, or bowing to political winds. Over the course of U.S. history, we can see empirical evidence that the judiciary does gauge public opinion, maintains ideological identification, and sometimes is tossed about by a political system in a state of flux. At this point, however, it can be only an a priori assumption that judicial selection shapes the kinds of decisions we get form judges. We must therefore take a look at what influences judicial decision making, and in turn the consequences of their decisions.

---

[24] Richard Watson & Ronald Downing (1969). The Politics of the Bench and the Bar: Judicial Selection under the Missouri Nonpartisan Court plan. John Wiley: NY. The authors contend that the politics of judicial selection shifted in Missouri to a concentration with the legal community. The plan did not lessen criticism of the methods either. Some of the traditional accusations concerning judicial selection such as it being political, drawing from certain strata of the legal profession, and not being egalitarian were leveled.

Judicial Decisions

Judges render most verdicts in the United States. While we have a right to trial by a jury, most cases are adjudicated through the plea bargaining process. Jury trials are a rarity. Judges in federal cases, particularly at the appellate level, are the only individuals to hear cases. Their work mirrors appellate judges at the state level. In the United States, judges routinely make decisions free from the scrutiny of others. Their decisions must be adhered to and have implications for how offenders are treated in the criminal justice system, as well as what civil rights and liberties will be enjoyed by the citizenry. What accounts for the variance in decision making at the appellate level in the judiciary? Why are some courts considered conservative and others liberal? What is the proper role of a judge?

Rational Actors

Lee Epstein and Jack Knight cogently describe in their award winning treatise on judicial decision making that judges are rational political actors who seek to make legal policy consistent with their "goals and interests."[25] Their assertion draws us closer to understanding judicial decisions from several perspectives. That these judges make decisions within the context of peers is an obvious perspective. They maintain policy positions and seek to pursue them through "strategic" decisions. The judiciary is a policy making institution within a system of checks and balances. Therefore, the number of "strategic" calculations any judge must make is substantial. Our attention, then, can be rightly placed on the "social

---

[25] Lee Epstein & Jack Knight (1998). The Choices Justices Make. CQ Press: Washington, D.C.

context" of judicial decision making along with the traditional explanations.[26]

Traditional explanations of judicial decisions center on legal explanations such as *stare decisis*. This legal doctrine is the practice of following precedent. Once cases are decided, precedents allow actors within the justice system to gauge and predict behavior of other actors. Precedent also becomes a standard by which cases and issues are decided. These views are more appropriately placed in a "traditional" view of decision making. We recognize that judges don't always follow precedent, and sometimes a majority of justices decide that precedents should be overturned.[27] As an issue in judicial process research, the law as a constraint upon judges has mixed evidence.[28] It does serve as a strategic consideration of judges.[29]

Most of the research on judicial decisions once viewed justices as insulated "mechanical" dispensers of the law that did not have personal preferences, ideologies, or attitudes about policy issues. Regardless of the explanations of how judges make decisions, we know that they do make them. We also know their decisions have implications for governance. What is important for us to know is that their decisions are

---

[26] For the most part, judicial decision making was based on legal explanations. See Edward Levi (1949). An Introduction to Legal Reasoning, University of Chicago Press: IL.
[27] Jeffrey Segal & Harold Spaeth (1996). The Influence of Stare Decisis on the Votes of United States Supreme Court Justices, American Journal of Political Science, v.40, pp. 971-1003.
[28] Healthy disagreement exists in the academic literature over what explains the decisions of judges. Special editions of journals have been dedicated to the many competing explanations.
[29] See Supra note 25.

real, are motivated by politics and ideology, and change behavior of other political actors.[30]

Social Context

Judges are influenced by interest groups and public opinion.[31] Interest groups can file what are known as amicus briefs that detail their position on the matters before the courts.[32] Justices use these briefs as a gauge of importance of the legal question and intensity with which positions are held by the parties involved. Judges realize with acuity that their decisions are watched by citizens and scrutinized by other political actors. In addition to making policies, they have a commitment to the institutional integrity of the court.[33]

Justices are also aware of the political environment. We discussed political environment earlier, but it is worth restating here in the context of judges. Typically, the classic model of politics views the political environment as the context for legislative behavior. Certainly, the political environment is also appropriate for judges, as well. In choosing whether to hear a case or not, for example, judges weigh the legal importance as well as the political and social aspects of the case. Amicus briefs are one way to judge these facets of a case, but they are by no means the only source of

---

[30] When Mitch McConnell argued on the Senate floor against campaign finance reform one of his issues was that the Supreme Court would invalidate the law. He later filed suit when the campaign finance law passed.

[31] See Supra note 25. Gregory Caldeira & Jack Knight (1988). Organized Interests and Agenda Setting in the U.S. Supreme Court, Vol. 82, American Political Science Review, pp. 1109-1127. J. Mondak & S. Smithey (1997). The Dynamics of Support for the Supreme Court. Journal of Politics, Vol. 59, pp. 1114-42.

[32] Amicus briefs are also known as friend of the court briefs.

[33] See Supra note 25.

information available to judges. They too read newspapers, travel abroad, associate with one another and other elite actors. Despite these interactions, judges and their work are somewhat of an enigma to the average citizen. The view that judges are hermit crabs is not based upon any known empirical evidence. Justices are very aware of social context when deciding to here a case or not.[34]

Despite the influence of social context on judicial decisions, and the fact that judges seek to move policy in a particular direction, and behave as strategically as other political actors in the pursuit of the interests, we have not yet delved into what difference the various accounts of decision making have for the kinds of outputs we derive from the judicial process. Before turning our attention to judicial policy making, we need to address some of the political considerations that affect the relationship of the court with other governing branches.

<u>Policy Drift</u>

Support for the court has typically been stable over time. There is some evidence which supports the suggestion that the court has higher popular support levels than other branches of government.[35] When the courts deviate from popular opinion or produces decisions that are outside the aggregate ideology of the other branches of government, they produce a "drift" policy. Drift is the distance between the ideological stripe of a judicial decision and the actual place on a liberal conservative continuum dictated by public opinion, control of Congress or the Presidency.

---

[34] H.W. Perry (1991). Deciding to Decide. Harvard University Press: MA.
[35] Thomas Marshall (1989). Public Opinion and the Supreme Court. Unwin-Hyman: MA.

Liberal and conservative observations of courts and court ideology are constructed by partisanship identity based on the appointing president or party label of the judge. In non-partisan elections, past political behavior, campaign contributions, and opinions usually point to partisanship and ideology. Over the history of the United States, due to the appointment process, political environment, and aggregate makeup of the courts, the judiciary has produced decisions that can be categorized as liberal or conservative. That is they expand or contract the reach of government in the area of economic regulation or relationship of the government and personal freedom. For the most part, courts tend to render decisions consistent with aggregate public opinion, as well as majority ideology in control of the other branches of government.

When justices make policy they seek to move policy in either a liberal or conservative direction. In the earlier chapter, we discussed the notion of restraint versus activism. Activism has usually been associated with liberal courts and liberal justices, but the term can be applied to conservative jurists, too. On the current court, Justices Souter and Scalia can be considered ideologues and activists. Some historical cases help us to better understand this idea of policy drift and ideology a bit clearer. Knowing that justices seek to make policy, that they are ideologues, that they act strategically, and are aware of social context and their place in the political environment can provide the proper lens for viewing court decisions and policy making.

Judicial Policy Making

The federal courts have typically been the place of refuge for minorities who sought to gain their civil rights and liberties. Some of the policies made through court decisions have been accepted, while others were seen as undermining popular control of government. In the Deep South, decisions that cleared the way for blacks to vote and attend white only schools were derided as the heavy hand of the federal government robbing sovereignty from the people. Depending upon which side of the ideological spectrum one places him or herself, judicial decisions can be viewed positively or negatively. We will now examine several cases that serve to place the courts in a social context.

Slavery

Slavery has been described as a stain on the history of the United States. Founders of the United States owned slaves, and some even struggled with the idea of freedom and equality for everyone. They also recognized the politically charged issue of slavery. Framers of the Constitution refused to even deal with the issue directly by carving out provisions outlining that slaves were not citizens even though their presence could count as three-fifths of a person. The Constitution put off the issue of deciding slavery questions until 1808.[36] Slavery eventually was the stimuli of the United States Civil War. More broadly, slavery repercussions still exist as all political issues related to discrimination have not been settled.[37]

Dredd Scott v. Sanford (1857) was perhaps the final political decision that contributed to the Civil War. Chief Justice Roger Taney predicted that the decision would settle the issue of slavery. Taney's exuberance was well-placed. The Supreme Court should have been the final arbiter on the issue.

---

[36] Article I enumerates the powers delegated to Congress. Population counts and citizenship issues related to slaves are contained there.
[37] Oprah Winfrey recently was denied access to an upscale French clothier. The sales clerk did not recognize her as the most powerful woman in the world. Accusations flew that only her race was recognized.

However, with a ruling that Dredd Scott was not a citizen of Missouri and could not bring the case to the Supreme Court because he was not a citizen and therefore not afforded protections of Congress or the courts, the Supreme Court settled the issue in terms of formal political pursuits.[38] Years later, fighting between southern and northern states ensued. African Americans would have to wait 100 more years to secure their rights and liberties with the courts.

Plessy v. Ferguson (1896)

Roughly forty years later, the courts had an additional opportunity to grant civil rights to blacks but declined to do so. In *Plessy v. Ferguson* (1896) the court articulated a "separate but equal doctrine" that held states could legally separate public accommodations on the basis of race. At the heart of the *Plessy* case was new amendments to the U.S. Constitution that guaranteed equal protection of laws and due process to those accused of violating laws. These amendments arising from the Civil War are known as the Civil War amendments.[39] The Court held that there was nothing inherently unequal about separate accommodations in the public sphere and therefore no Constitutional prohibitions had been violated.

Sixty years later in *Brown v. Board of Education* (1954), the Supreme Court overturned *Plessy*. The *Brown* case dealt with school segregation. Unlike Deep South segregation which was embodied in Jim Crow laws, the courts also found Constitutional violations based on segregation by practice. The former type is overt, while the latter is a bit more subtle.

---

[38]Findlaw.com is legal database containing a written opinion in *Dredd Scott v. Stanford (1857)*.

[39] The 13th, 14th, and 15th Amendments constitute the Civil War Amendments.

In a forceful unanimous decision, the court laid the groundwork for subsequent civil right's expansions in the areas of voting rights, access to housing, education, and access to credit.

Between *Brown* and *Plessy*, the courts had other opportunities to decide cases involving the freedoms of individuals and conveyance of justice. During World War II, the courts decided that the internment of Japanese Americans did not violate their Constitutional rights. In a time of war, both Congress and the President have a duty to protect. In what amounted to a denial of due process, using round ups, imprisonment, registration, and curfews, the United States systematically abridged the rights of many natural born citizens based on nothing more than race. Congress has since granted reparations to the Japanese Americans and apologized.[40] The courts once again abdicated its responsibility to spread civil liberties to a broad population of citizens.

Warren Court Era (1953-1969)

Court eras are named after the Chief Justice presiding at the time of the decisions. During the Warren Court Era, the Supreme Court incorporated much of the Bill of Rights upon the states. Nationalization of the Bill of Rights began roughly in the 1930's with cases dealing with right to an attorney. The most notable case is *Powell v. Alabama* (1932) which is also known as the Scottsboro Boys case. Nine black males were accused of raping two white women while all of them were hitching a ride on a freight train. Without the availability of an attorney, the accused were convicted and sentenced to death.

---

[40] Civil Liberties Act of 1988. This created restitution for World War II internment of Japanese-Americans and Aleuts, as well as apologized for the atrocities.

In this case, the Supreme Court held that the Constitution does grant due process and in this case it had been violated. Thus began a series of cases involving the expansion of civil liberties and rights including the *Brown* case already referenced.

Some of the notable cases decided during the Warren Era include *Brown*, and also *Miranda v. Arizona*, *Gideon v. Wainwright*, and *Mapp v. Ohio*. In addition to the rapid expansion of the rights of the accused, the Warren Court also upheld and forced other federal courts to enforce the Civil Rights Act of 1964, Voting Rights Act 1965, and Fair Housing Act 1968. These cases routinely sided with citizens who had been disfranchised by government power and abuses. Subsequent decisions by the federal courts have expanded civil rights to include prohibitions of sexual harassment while upholding controversial policies such as affirmative action.[41]

Post Warren

Contemporary political struggles over the judiciary revolve around whether the courts have expanded civil rights and liberties too far.[42] Nothing stirs debate such as issues of abortion and school prayer or the establishment clause of the Constitution. The courts have been fairly unclear on what constitutes an establishment of religion. Pro-lifers seethe over *Roe v. Wade*. Liberals still bemoan the outcome of *Bush v. Gore* (2000) whereby the Supreme Court decided who would become President of the United States. Most recently, the War

---

[41] *Meritor v. Vinson* (1986) established sexual harassment as a form of workplace discrimination. Lyndon Johnson issued an executive order that established affirmative action. Some cases involving affirmative action are *Griggs v. Duke Power*, *U.S. Steel v. Weber*, *Bakke v. California Board of Regents*. The University of Michigan Cases.

[42] For a scathing critique of the expansion of civil liberties see H. Rothwax (1996). Guilty: The Collapse of Criminal Justice. Warner Books: NY.

on Terrorism has spawned new controversies revolving around the USA PATRIOT ACT and how to balance liberty and security. Recent retirements of justices and continued judiciary vacancies continue to promote the struggle.

Summary

The judiciary has substantial gravity in the dispensing of justice. Over the course of United States history, it has been the courts that have protected minority rights while preserving majority rule. At some points in history, like the Antebellum Era, the Civil Rights Era, and the New Deal Era, the courts positive and negative actions have hindered the progress of society. Why the courts failed to consistently interpret the law with predictability is obvious.Judges and the judicial branch are policy makers within a system of shared governance. Not only are the decisions of judges strategically calculated to achieve the best possible outcomes in relation to their own agendas and interests, but the administration of justice is often politicized. We should not reasonably expect anything different than politicized jurisprudence given the political struggles over judicial selection, the context in which decisions are made, and the sense of place judges feel when their decisions lead to policy shifts.

We are now left to entertain the idea of whether or not the judicial branch, with judges at the center, can properly discharge its duties when a level of politics naturally leaches into the system. Despite the judiciary's strength, it is still somewhat limited in absolute power. Other than incarceration and monetary awards, the judiciary requires others to ensure compliance with its decisions. This had led some to conclude that there are limits as to what the courts can do, including delivering justice with predictability. Our conclusion concerning whether or not politics hinders the judiciary is that politics has a permanent role. As de Tocqueville observed, political questions eventually become legal questions. Politics permeates the selection of judges, the agenda of the court, judicial decisions, and implementation of rulings. We tend not to err on the side of extremism with our view of the judiciary. The judiciary manages legal conflict politically. Politics is the most readily available tool for resolving disputes. Justice will sometimes be scarified due to politics, but not always. Politicized justice is the price we pay for popular control of government.

Chapter Six Rights of the Accused

The balance between liberty and security has been debated since the birth of this Nation. While the "authors of the U.S. Constitution (1787) believed they could create in a written document a perfect balance between security and liberty, goals expressed in the Preamble as to "insure the domestic tranquility" and secure the blessings of liberty,"[1] this was not the case. Citizens insisted that a Bill of Rights (1791) be incorporated which limits the rights of the government in the enforcement of the criminal law.[2] It is important to recognize that "the Bill of Rights offered citizens protection only against the federal government. Over the years, the procedural safeguards of most of the provisions of the Bill of Rights have been applied to the actions of the state governments through the fourteenth amendment (and states are free to grant even more protection than is required by the federal Constitution)."[3] With respect to the Bill of Rights, criminal justice professionals did not take them seriously until the 1960's. Under the leadership of Chief Justice Earl Warren, the United States Supreme Court actively and aggressively fought to ensure that the individual rights guaranteed in the Bill of Rights were not empty promises. Ultimately, the Warren Court (1953-1969) is responsible for numerous landmark decisions that assist in the administration of justice in the

---

[1] Joel Samaha (2006). Criminal Justice. 7th (ed). P.25. Thomson/Wadsworth, Belmont, CA.
[2] Id.
[3] Larry Gaines & Roger Leroy Miller (2006). Criminal Justice in Action: The Core. p.89. Thomson/Wadsworth. Belmont, CA.

twenty-first century.[4] While this is a noble cause, we must be cognizant that the administration of justice in the United States is far from perfect. Law enforcement officers, judges, prosecutors and defense attorneys often engage in distributive and bargain basement justice.[5] In reality, the actions of these professionals are in direct contrast to the Bill of Rights. In reality, is the criminal justice system in search for the truth regarding those accused of crimes? According to Rothwax (1996), "our system is a carefully crafted maze, constructed of elaborate and impenetrable barriers to the truth."[6] This chapter operates on the premise that there are two types of justice in the United States (those for the elite and non-elite). To restate, citizens only have as many rights as they can afford. This is consistent with our theoretical theme that public policies are created by the moneyed elites which serve their own individual interests. The focus of this chapter is to examine germane issues which undermine the "Bill of Rights" (see Table 6-1). Specifically, this chapter discusses the USA PATRIOT ACT, indigent offender systems, adversarial illusion, jury impartiality and excessive bail.

---

[4] *Mapp v. Ohio*, 367 U.S. 643, *Gideon v. Wainwright*, 372 U.S. 335, *Mallory v. Hogan*, 378 U.S. 1, *Escobedo v. Illinois*, 378 U.S. 478, *Pointer v. Texas*, 380 U.S. 400, *Parker v. Gladden*, 385 U.S. 363, *Miranda v. Arizona*, 384 U.S. 436, *Klopfer v. North Carolina*, 386 U.S. 21, *In re Guilt*, 387 U.S. 1, *Duncan v. Louisianan*, 391 U.S. 145, *Benton v. Maryland*, 395 U.S. 784.

[5] Harold J. Rothwax (1996). Guilty: The Collapse of Criminal Justice. Warner Books. New York, NY.

[6] Id. pp. 18-19.

Table 6-1: Constitutional Amendments (Bill of Rights) Germane to the Criminal Justice System

Right Guaranteed	Amendment
Right against unreasonable searches and seizures	4th
Right against arrest without probable cause	4th
Right against self incrimination	5th
Right against double jeopardy	5th
Right to due process of law	5th
Right to a speedy trial	6th
Right to a jury trial	6th
Right to know the charges	6th
Right to cross examine witnesses	6th
Right to an attorney	6th
Right to compel witness's on one's behalf	6th
Right against excessive bail	8th
Right against excessive fines	8th
Right against cruel and unusual punishment	8th

Source: United States Constitution: Bill of Rights.

USA PATRIOT ACT (4th and 5th Amendment)

September 11, 2001 will be a day the United States will remember. Close to 3,000 individuals died when Al Qaeda terrorist hijacked four commercial airliners and crashed into the World Trade Centers in New York City, the Pentagon in Washington DC, and Somerset County, Pennsylvania (the target was Washington, DC). Instantly, President Bush declared to the world, "that the United States was formally engaged in a war against terrorism."[7] Prior to this act, however, "the United States had been in an undeclared war against terror for decades prior to September 2001. Specifically, three presidential administrations, republican (Ronald Regan, 1981-1989, George H. Bush, 1989-1993 and Democrat Bill Clinton, 1993-2001) had to respond to attacks against Americans both at home and abroad, carried out for the most part by small numbers of foreign extremist religious groups who had declared a holy war against the United States."[8] It is precisely the small number of individuals or groups "quantity factor" that has bewildered the Bush administration. Specifically, the United States is engaged in asymmetrical warfare.[9] In search for a panacea, the Bush Administration, on October 26, 2001, with virtually no debate among Congress, signed the USA PATRIOT Act (United and Strengthening America by Providing Appropriate Tools Required to Intercept and Obstruct Terrorism).[10] Citizens should be cognizant that this act undermines the balance between national security and personal freedoms of Americans. The fourth amendment protects against

---

[7] Howard Ball (2004). The USA Patriot Act. p.2. ABC-CLIO: Santa Barbara, CA.

[8] Id. p. 33. Jonathan White (2002). Terrorism: An Introduction. Wadsworth:Thomson. Belmont, CA.

[9] Howard Bell (2004). The USA Patriot Act. pp. 225-226. "Asymmetric warfare: in the modern age of global terrorism, wars can be fought not just between nation-states but also between a nation-state and terrorist groups or cells, individuals who are not agents or combatants of a nation-state. The U.S. war on terrorism, for example, pits a major nation against a very small number of Islamic fundamentalist led by an individual, Osama bin Laden, who does not act on behalf of a nation-state. Hence the asymmetry in this type of war; millions of military personnel with the latest hardware versus small bands of zealots who do not have weapons to match their mightier foe".

[10] USA PATRIOT ACT. October 26, 2001. Public Law 107-56.

unreasonable searches and seizures, however, the Patriot Act, "substantially increases the investigatory authority of federal, state, and local police agencies. The act permits longer jail terms for certain suspects arrested without a warrant, broadens "sneak and peak" search authority (searches conducted without prior notice and in the absence of the suspect) and enhances the power of prosecutors."[11] This act further increases the ability of federal authorities to tap phones (including wireless devices) and track Internet usage.[12] Civil libertarians are concerned that the Patriot Act will be used to further infringe on American's civil liberties. In essence, the United States Constitution has been compromised and the citizenry is concerned, "that the act makes it too easy for law enforcement agents and prosecutors to gather evidence."[13] Since the passage of the Patriot Act, newspapers such as the New York Times, the Houston Chronicle and the Washington Post have questioned the integrity of the Act. Moreover, numerous legislators such as Larry Craig (R-IN), John Sununu (R-NH), Lisa Murkowski (R-AK), Ron Wyden (D-OR), Richard Durbin (D-IL), and former Georgia Republican Bob Barr, chairman of "Patriots to Restore Checks and Balances" have spoken out in opposition. In addition, the United States General Accounting Office and Office of Inspector General, as well as "hundreds of pressure groups, have condemned the law because of its capacity to diminish civil liberties protections in the name of national security against terrorism."[14] As for the citizenry, a recent Gallup Poll "Liberty

---

[11] Frank Schmalleger (2005). Criminal Justice Today: An Introductory Text for the 21st Century. p. 312. Pearson: Prentice Hall, Upper Saddle lakes, NJ.
[12] Id.
[13] See Supra note 3 at p. 403
[14] Howard Ball (2004). The USA PATRIOT ACT. ABC-CLIO. p.70. Santa Barbara, CA.

vs. Security: Public Mixed on Patriot Act" reports that 78% of Americans who are somewhat familiar with the Patriot Act believe it goes too far in restricting civil liberties.[15] To put this figure into perspective, as of April (2005), "five states and 372 counties, cities, villages and towns have passed resolutions, ordinances or ballot initiatives condemning the law created by Constitution-crushing former Attorney General John Ashcroft and expressing their commitment to the values expressed in the Bill of Rights."[16] What is the future of the Patriot Act? The following quotes may reveal the answer: "freedom and fear are at war" George W. Bush, September 11, 2001
and "this Administration is using fear as a political tool" Al Gore, November 9, 2003.

Indigent Offender Systems (6th Amendment)

Americans often remark "you get what you pay for?" Does this sentiment apply to indigent defense services? While the cornerstone of American Jurisprudence is equity, due process and justice, do citizens who are unable to hire private counsel suffer in and out of the courtroom? It should be noted, that the majority of citizens who are charged with a crime are unable to obtain private counsel. Of course, those individuals who do not have economic resources will be assigned representation.[17]

---

[15] Gallup Poll News Service: The Gallup Organization. (2005, July 19). Liberty vs. Security: Public Mixed on patriot Act.

[16] John Nichols (2005). Better SAFE than Sorry Patriot Act. Madison.com.

[17] Leading Constitutional cases pertaining to the right to counsel are: *Powell v. Alabama,* 287 U.S. 45 (1932) (counsel appointed for poor, illiterate or ignorant defendants in state capital cases), *Johnson v. Zerbst,* 304 U.S. 458 (1938) (counsel appointed in federal cases for trial only; not appeal), *Betts v. Brady,* 316 U.S. 455 (1942) (counsel appointed in state cases under special circumstances), *Gideon v. Wainwright,* 372 U.S. 335 (1963) (counsel appointed in state felony cases), *Argersinger v. Hamlin,*

Just how much do attorneys cost? The cost is often arbitrarily dictated by the type and complexity of the case, the attorney's years of practice, and past successes. In a study conducted by the Bureau of Statistics, "over 80% of felony defendants charged with a violent crime in the country's largest counties and 66% in the U.S. district courts have publicly financed attorneys.[18] Currently, there are several ways for delivering public defense services: the staff public defender model, the assigned counsel model, and the contract model.[19] It should be noted that the public defender model is the primary method in delivering indigent services. As for the administration of indigent services by the various states, there exist two primary methods: state wide or county and regional level.[20] As with most facets of the criminal justice system, there exist many

---

407 U.S. 25 (1972) (counsel appointed in cases involving misdemeanors that are punishable by over six months of incarceration).

[18] Caroline Harlow (November 2000). Defense Counsel in Criminal Cases. Bureau of Justice Statistics: Special Report. Washington, DC.

[19] Improving Criminal Justice Systems Through Expanded Strategies And Innovative Collaborations (March 2000). Report of the National Symposium on Indigent Defense.

[20] According to National Center for State Courts (2005) (ncsconline.org) Statewide public defender Systems (sixteen states): Alaska, Colorado, Connecticut, Delaware, Hawaii, Maryland, Massachusetts, Minnesota, Missouri, New Hampshire, New Jersey, New Mexico, Rhode Island, Vermont, Wisconsin and Wyoming. States with an indigent defense commission that sets guidelines for the provision of indigent defense services statewide (twelve states) (local jurisdictions decides which delivery model to use i.e. public defender, assigned counsel or contract): Arkansas, Georgia, Indiana, Kansas, Kentucky, Louisiana, Nebraska, North Dakota, Ohio, Oklahoma, South Carolina, and Tennessee. As for counties and regional systems (Fourteen states): Alabama, Arizona, California, Idaho, Maine, Michigan, Mississippi, Montana, New York, North Carolina, South Dakota, Texas, Utah, and Washington. There are nine states in which the state or county and region deliver systems: District

issues relating to the use of indigent defense attorneys. To begin, "public offenders are often overworked. In the Florida counties of Orange and Osceola, public defenders handle about 750 cases a year, more than five times their recommended caseload. Sometimes, there are not enough lawyers to meet the needs of poor defendants. In Riverside County, California, twelve thousand indigent defendants each year plead guilty without ever speaking to a lawyer. In Oregon thousands of nonviolent misdemeanor and low-level felony cases are dismissed due to lack of available court appointed attorneys."[21] Another issue of concern is the compensation of court appointed or public defenders. As for court appointed attorneys, the state of Alabama, "pays $40 an hour for out-of court preparation and $60 an hour for time in court. Considering the wages from private clients that these lawyers lose every hour they work for the state, an Alabama defense attorney who spends an average amount of time preparing for a death penalty case is being paid less than the national minimum wage."[22] Moreover, in the state of Virginia, "the most a court appointed attorney can be paid to work on a non-capital charge with a punishment of more than twenty years in prison is $1,235."[23] As for public defenders, the annual salary is incredibly low (see Table 6-2).

---

of Columbia, Florida, Illinois, Iowa, Nevada, Oregon, Pennsylvania, Virginia, and West Virginia.

[21] See Supra note 3 at pp. 212-213. Also see Bill Rankin (March, 24, 2003). "Right to a Lawyer Still Not a Given for Poor Defendants".

[22] Id. p. 212. Dallas County Attorneys Consider Strike on Indigent Cases. Associated Press News wire. February 26, 2002.

[23] Id. p. 212.

Table 6- 2: Annual Salary of Assistant Public Defenders

State	Minimum
Alaska	$45,000
Colorado	$35,124
Connecticut	$41,612
Delaware	$36,000
Iowa	$35,152
Massachusetts	$28,600
Missouri	$30,500
New Hampshire	$31,018
New Jersey	$40,965
New Mexico	$28,941
Rhode Island	$38,000
Vermont	$29,500
West Virginia	$32,000
Wisconsin	$37,087

Source: Carol DeFrances (September 2001). State Funded Indigent Defense Services (1999). Bureau of Justice Statistics. U.S. Department of Justice.

As the above salaries indicate, the question warrants "are we getting what we paid for?" Or to restate, "Are defendants getting what they deserve?" According to a report by the NCAAP Legal Defense and Educational Fund (2003), Mississippi's indigent offenders are victimized by "an outdated and broken down system of justice."[24] Interestingly, "the state of Mississippi does not contribute one dollar towards the representation of poor defendants. Instead it requires counties to shoulder the full obligation of providing

[24] National Legal Defense and Educational Fund (2003). Assembly Line Justice: Mississippi's Indigent Defense Crisis.

lawyers for the poor. It is an obligation that many counties cannot or will not honor."[25] As a result:

- In some counties, an indigent defendant may wait up to a full year before he has his first conversation about his case with a court appointed lawyer.
- Children as young as 14 are locked up in adult jails where they wait months to speak with a lawyer.
- Many lawyers for the poor never meet their clients until the day of trial.
- Meetings between lawyer and client are brief, and often take place in the courtroom, just minutes before critical hearings.
- Lawyers for the poor lack the funds to conduct the most basic investigation, to conduct legal research, or to hire experts. In many counties, hiring an investigator or a psychiatrist in a non-death penalty case is only possible if the lawyer pays for it out of his or her own pocket.[26]

Another state in need of indigent defense improvement is Texas. According to the Texas Appleseed Fair Defense Project (2000), "previous research and investigation by others have demonstrated that serious indigent defense failures occur in the state with alarming frequency."[27] Upon examining indigent representation in 23 counties which comprise 61% of the Texas population, the study revealed:

---

[25] Id. p.6.
[26] Id. p.6.
[27] Texas Appleseed Fair Defense Project (December, 2000). The Fair Defense Report: Analysis of Indigent Defense Practices in Texas. p.1

- Throughout the state, many county criminal justice systems are set up to discourage trials and encourage plea agreements, even when meritorious issues may be in question.
- According to a private attorney in Harris County, " if you're in custody, you can get a fairly quick trial, but pleading's the fastest way to go." This attorney has not gone to trial in five years.[28]

The future of indigent defendants in the United States is at best depressing. The majority of states have and continue to devote little resources to rectify this asymmetry. Issues such as high case volume, unjust compensation and plea bargaining will ensure that innocent defendants will be imprisoned.

Adversarial Illusion (6th Amendment)

American television and movies depict the criminal courtroom as a battleground where two passionate advocates are fighting for their cause (state v. defendant) in front of a neutral judge and impartial jury of twelve. Moreover, there is often a "Perry Mason" moment in these fictional accounts. Attorneys often suggest they're in search of "the truth." However, these characterizations are far from accurate. For example:

- Capital defendant George McFarland's lawyer John Benn slept through much of his 1992 trail. "His mouth kept falling open and his head lolled back on his shoulders… again and again and again and again" writes a newspaper reporter. "It's boring" the lawyer told the judge. But the constitutional right to counsel was not violated, according to the trial judge, because

[28] Id. p.34.

"[t]he Constitution does not say the lawyer has to be awake". The Texas Court of Criminal Appeals upheld McFarland's death sentence, and the U.S. Supreme Court denied review."[29]

The previous example is incongruent with the general public's perception of the American courtroom Defense attorneys are instructed to zealously defend their client within the boundaries of the law: how do we quantify a zealous defense? Moreover, how do we quantify whether or not the attorney effectively represented his or her client? There are numerous accounts of defendants who claim their attorney sold them out. In reality, the majority of citizens can not afford due process. The celebrated cases of William Kennedy Smith, Claus von Bulow, O.J. Simpson, Scott Peterson and Kobe Bryant have distorted the reality of day to day jurisprudence for Americans. In the above cases, "the defendant had an extremely skilled and highly paid team of attorneys as well as trial consultants, investigators and public relations specialist."[30] The overwhelming majority of criminal defendants do not have substantial bankrolls to defend themselves in a court of law. Roughly two out of ten defendants will hire private counsel.[31] While the celebrated cases are few and far between, the daily life of a defense attorney is not glamorous. In all actuality, the last place an attorney wants to be is in a trial. According to a district judge in Dallas "attorneys want to be appointed to jail

---

[29] Improving Criminal Justice Systems through Expanded Strategies and Innovative Collaborations (March, 2000). Report of the National Symposium on Indigent Defense. p.6. Washington, DC.
[30] Joycelyn Pollock (2004). Ethics in Crime and Justice. p. 235. Thomson: Wadsworth. Belmont, CA.
[31] Defense Counsel in Criminal Cases (2000). Bureau of Justice Statistics: Special Report.

revocations and pleas. This is where the money is-it's not in trials."[32] To further complicate the image of the defense attorney, research conducted by Blumberg's (1967) suggests attorneys are double agents.[33] Specifically, "both prosecutor and defense attorney conspire to appear as something they are not-adversaries in a do-or-die situation. What is more commonly the case is that the prosecutor and the defense attorney will still be working together when the client is gone; thus their primary allegiance is not to the client, but to themselves."[34] In fact, "accused persons come and go in the court system schema, but the structure and its occupational incumbents remain to carry on their respective career, occupational and organizational enterprises."[35] Given the above, citizens i.e. defendants, should be concerned with the administration of justice in the United States. There is a double standard that is masked by an illusion.

Jury Impartiality (6th Amendment)

When the state and the defendant are unable to reach a plea bargain, a group of twelve jurors are given the responsibility to determine whether the state proved their case beyond a reasonable doubt.[36] In theory, these jurors are expected to be impartial; however this is not plausible or realistic. Trial

---

[32] Texas Appleseed Fair Defense Project. The Fair Defense Report: Analysis of Indigent Defense Practices in Texas. December (December, 2000).
[33] Abraham Blumberg (June, 1967). The Practice of Law as Confidence Game: Organization Co-Optation of a Profession. Law and Society Review. In George Cole, Marc Gertz & Amy Bunger (2004). The Criminal Justice System: Politics and Policies. Thomson: Wadsworth. Belmont, CA.
[34] Joycelyn Pollock (2004) Ethics in Crime and Justice. pp.232- 233. Thomson; Wadsworth. Belmont,CA.
[35] See Supra note 31. p. 241.
[36] *Williams v. Florida*, 399 U.S. 780, (1970).

attorneys do not want jurors who are impartial.[37] An attorney worth his or her salt will do everything in their power to select jurors who are partial to his or her client's case. Attorneys attempt this task either through an oral or written questionnaire.[38] Either method should attempt to ascertain two types of information: demographic and individual differences (personality, attitudes and ideologies). Examples of demographic information include age, race, marital status, education, income, and occupation. Examples of individual differences are an individual's personality (extraverted and conscientious),[39] attitudes (regarding capital punishment or religion) or ideologies (authoritarianism or dogmatism). The assumption is that through examining this information, attorneys will be able to deselect potential threatening jurors.[40] Attorneys, whose clients are wealthy enough, often utilize jury consultants to

---

[37] Jeremy Barber (1994). The Jury is Still Out. American Criminal Law Review. Vol. 31, pp.1225-1252.

[38] In all states, jurors must meet certain criteria in order to serve on a jury. On a given jury week (typically Monday morning), a judge will go through an orientation with all citizens who have been summoned for jury service. To be eligible to serve on a jury, citizens must be: a citizen of the United States, over eighteen years of age, free from felony convictions, in good health, intelligent enough to understand issues that may come up in trial, comprehend the English language i.e. read and write and have resided within the jurisdiction for at least one year.

[39] Personality is understood by measuring five dimensions (extraversion, neuroticism, agreeableness, conscientiousness, and openness). For more see L. Goldberg (1990). An alternative Description of personality: The big five structure. Journal of Personality and Social Psychology. Vol. 59, pp.1216-1229.

[40] The process of eliminating jurors is either challenges for cause or peremptory strikes. Each side (state and defense) are allowed a specific number. Peremptory challenges are controversial. For more information see *Batson v. Kentucky,* 476 U.S. 79 (1986). *J.E.B. v. Alabama EX Rel. T.B*, 511 U.S. 127.

assist in this process. The trial consultant industry is estimated to be worth four-hundred million dollars a year. Even after a jury is selected, attorneys must be cognizant that when jurors cross the threshold of the courtroom, they are not going to leave their life experiences outside the court. To demonstrate, jurors may be influenced by extralegal factors rather than the facts or strength of evidence pertaining to the case at hand. For example, research demonstrates that jurors are affected by a defendant's physical attractiveness.[41] During the (1994) murder trial of Eric and Lyle Menendez, jurors claimed they did not believe the brothers had killed their parents because the boys looked like nice young men.[42] Another example of an extralegal factor that influences a juror is social categorization. This occurs when a juror views others as either belonging to their own group (in group) or another group (out group).[43] Interestingly, social categorization is based on basic demographics (age, race and gender). Given the above, it is obvious that the impartial juror is not realistic. At the same time, there are no perfect jurors. Attorneys and defendants must recognize that even after the deselecting process there are social psychological factors that may influence a juror. Ultimately, readers of this text should understand that the right to an impartial jury, found in the Sixth Amendment, is null and void.

---

[41] W.A. Castellow, K.L. Wuensch & C.H. Moore (1990). Effects of Physical Attractiveness of the Plaintiff and Defendant in Sexual Harassment Judgments. Vol. 5, Journal Social Behavior and Personality.

[42] Craig Parks & Lawrence Sanna (1998). Group Performance and Interaction. Westview Press. Boulder: CO.

[43] Robert Baron & Donn Byrne (1997). Social Psychology. Thomson: Wadsworth. Belmont, CA.

Excessive Bail (8th Amendment)

While the Eighth Amendment provides for bail, "the amendment does not guarantee the right to bail.[44] Instead it states that excessive bail shall not be required."[45] The purpose of bail is to ensure reappearance of the accused and prevent the un-convicted from suffering imprisonment unnecessarily.[46] In determining whether to grant bail, judicial authorities often rely on a variety of criteria.

According to Samaha (2006) the criteria are:

- The seriousness of the current charge.
- The criminal history of the defendant.
- Strength of the prosecution's case.[47]

Determining whether to grant bail is often a controversial issue for judicial authorities. At present, "there is no uniform system for pretrial detention; each jurisdiction has its own bail tariffs, or general guidelines concerning the proper amount of bail. For misdemeanors, the police usually follow a pre-approved bail schedule created by local judicial authorities. In felony cases, the primary responsibility to set bail lies with the judge."[48] While defendants are innocent until proven guilty, we must recognize that our district and

---

[44] Bail is the release of a defendant prior to his or her trial.
[45] See Supra note 3 at p. 221.
[46] Frank Schmalleger (2005). Criminal Justice Today: An Introductory Text for the 21st Century. Pearson: Prentice Hall. Upper Saddle Lakes, NJ.
[47] See Supra note 1.
[48] See Supra note 3 at pp. 222-223.

circuit judges are elected officials who need the communities support if reelection is sought. Given this, a defendant may receive a high bail or a denial. As for bail amounts, Table 6-3 demonstrates the median bail for violent, property, drug and public order crimes.

Table 6-3: Median Bail Amounts for Felony Defendants in 75 of the Largest Counties

Type of Crime	Median Bail Amount
Violent	
Murder	$250,000
Rape	$25,000
Robbery	$25,000
Assault	$10,000
Property	
Burglary	$15,000
Larceny/theft	$5,000
Motor vehicle theft	$10,000
Forgery	$5,000
Fraud	$5,000
Drug Offenses	
Trafficking	$10,000
Other drug	$10,000
Public Order Offenses	
Weapons	$7,500
Driving related	$5,000
other public order	$5,000

Source: Gerald Rainville & Brian Reaves (2003). Felony Defendants in large Urban Counties, 2000. Bureau of Justice Statistics. U.S. Department of Justice.

As the above illustrates, there are considerable differences among the various offenses and bail amounts.

Ultimately, we must ask, "is the Eighth Amendment's guarantee against excessive bail undermined by race, gender, or economic status?" See Table 6-4.

Table 6-4: Gender, Race, and Conviction Status

	Percent of Jail Inmates	
Characteristic	2000	2004
Total	100%	100%
Gender		
Male	88.1%	87.7%
Female	11.9%	12.3%
Race		
White	43.6%	44.4%
Black	39.2%	38.6%
Hispanic	15.4%	15.2%
Other	1.8%	1.8%
Conviction Status		
Convicted	39.4%	39.7%
Male	34.7%	34.8%
Female	4.7%	4.9%
Un-convicted	60.6%	60.3%
Male	53.5%	53.0%
Female	7.1%	7.3%

Source: Paige Harrison & Allen Beck (2005). Prison and Jail Inmates at Midyear 2004. Bureau of Justice Statistics. U.S. Department of Justice.

As the above indicates, an alarming 60% of jail occupants are un-convicted. This translates to approximately

400,000 individuals.[49] The research raises the question: If these defendants are in jail, how can they assist in preparing for their defense? According to Lester (2005), "The difference between being released prior to trial and being incarcerated is often the difference between an acquittal and a conviction. No matter how quickly a case is fast-tracked through the system, a detained defendant will suffer some material harm. The defendant will be displaced from work and familial duties, as well as suffer the stigma of being a prisoner. But most importantly, a freed defendant is able to better defend himself against the government. A freed defendant can better assist his attorney in gathering evidence and securing witnesses so that the government's burden to convict remains high. Pretrial detention severely limits a defendant's ability to defend themselves simply because their ability to contact the world is necessarily restricted."[50] To illustrate:

- On November 9, 2001, Shirley Johnson of Mobile, Alabama was gambling at a casino in Gulfport, Mississippi. She allegedly attempted to take $200.00 in quarters that came out of a slot machine into which she had not put any money. A casino security guard stopped her and the police were called. Ms. Johnson was arrested for violating Mississippi's gaming control act and taken to the Harrison County Jail. More than seven months after her arrest, she remained in jail. Although her bail was $100.00, she could not afford to pay it. No attorney visited her or argued for release on her own recognizance. On June 17, 2002, Johnson

---

[49] Paige Harrison & Allen Beck (2005). Prison and Jail Inmates at Midyear 2004. Bureau of Justice Statistics. U.S. Department of Justice.
[50] Joseph Lester (2005). Presumed Innocent, Freed Dangerous: The Eighth Amendments Right to Bail. Northern Kentucky University Law Review. 32 N. Ky.L. Rev. 1.

came before a judge and pled guilty. She was sentenced to time served plus one year of probation. The cost of her 220 days of incarceration was $6,820.00, all paid for by the county.[51]

Summary

The rights of offenders should not be undermined by ambitious politicians or incompetent justice professionals. The United States is based on the foundation of providing citizens basic rights against the government. At present, The USA PATRIOT ACT is threatening some of these guarantees. The indigent offender system throughout the country is not uniform. There exist many offenders who lack economic resources to adequately defend themselves in a court of law. As a consequence, these offenders are victimized by a society who pleads "no money". Even more disconcerting is the illusion that the criminal court is adversarial. Far too often, do our judges and attorneys really care about the search for the truth? Ultimately, these courtroom actors are restricted by organizational and political parameters. With respect to the impartial jury, this is impossible. Jurors are from all walks of life. These men and women bring in the courtroom their beliefs, attitudes, ideologies and personalities. Last, the number of persons in jail who have not been convicted is alarming. The innocent until proven guilty standard appears to have lost its meaning.

---

[51] National Legal Defense and Educational Fund (2003). Assembly Line Justice. Mississippi Indigent Defense Crisis.

Chapter Seven Politics of Punishment

When an individual has committed a crime against society he/she will be punished.[1] Ultimately, United States citizens should question the justifications and validity i.e. purpose of punishment? Is the purpose to inflict great harm on the individual or protect society? Additionally, if two individuals receive the same punishment, are they equally affected by that punishment? Moreover, if two citizens from the same state commit the same crime will they receive the same punishment (sentence)? Are citizens treated fairly by judicial authorities who administer punishments? Do race, gender and economic status affect the judge's decision? Interestingly, "philosophers have long debated why a wrongful act should be punished. Many social scientists suggest that criminal punishment maintains and defends the social order. By threatening potential law violators and by making the lives of violators uncomfortable, they say, punishments reduce the likelihood of future or continued criminal behavior."[2] To counter, is it possible that by making the lives of law violators uncomfortable, society will only anger and frustrate the offenders to a point that, when released into society, the individuals will engage in instrumental and/or expressive crimes?[3] In the United States, contemporary punishments i.e.

---

[1] Given that he or she is apprehended and found guilty in a court of law (of course some offenders may plea bargain).
[2] Frank Schmalleger & John Smykla (2005). Corrections in the 21st Century. p. 73. McGraw Hill. New York, NY.
[3] Expressive crimes are crimes such as murder or rape. Ultimately, the offender expresses his/her rage, anger or frustration on a victim. Instrumental crimes are crimes such as robbery or theft. For more information see: Marvin Wolfgang (1958). Patterns in Criminal Homicide.

sentences, are carried out either in prison (incarceration) or the community. As for which punishment (prison or community) is more likely to deter offenders from committing additional crimes, it appears "neither works."[4] A recidivism study conducted by Langan and Levin (2002) found that, "67.5% of the prisoners released from prison were rearrested for a new offense within three years of their release."[5] As for probation, "most studies have found that one-fifth to one-third of probationers fail to abide by the terms of their probation."[6] Given these statistics, it appears that the criminal justice system has a serious problem. To begin, our prisons are not correcting, our community based programs are struggling and offenders are being sentenced to prison and community based programs at record paces. Are we as a society failing ourselves as well as those who have committed crimes? In reality, our society will never be utopian. There will always be citizens who commit acts against individuals i.e. society. As a society, citizens should question the integrity and the process of punishment. To begin, judicial authorities are increasingly losing their discretion in matters of sentencing

---

Philadelphia: University of Pennsylvania Press. S. Fesbach (1964). The Function of Aggression and the Regulation of Aggressive Drive. Psychological Review, 71, pp. 257-272.

[4] Neither work is a play on the infamous "nothing works" by Robert Martinson (1975). What Works: Questions and Answers about Prison Reform. Public Interest, No. 35 (1974). pp. 22-54. See: Douglas Lipton, Robert Martinson and Judith Wilkes (1975). The Effectiveness of Correctional Treatment: A Survey of Treatment Evaluation Studies. Praeger:NY.

[5] Patrick Langan & David Levin (June, 2002). Recidivism of Prisoners Released in 1994. Bureau of Justice Statistics. U.S. Department of Justice. Also, M. Geerken and H. Hayes (1993). Probation and Parole: Public Risks and the Future of Incarceration Alternatives. Criminology, 31, pp. 549-564.

[6] Todd Clear & Harry Dammer (2003). The Offender in the Community. p. 292. Thomson: Wadsworth. Belmont, CA.

(punishing).[7] Ultimately, this decrease in discretion is a result of political leader's involvement in punishment. The purpose of this chapter is to demonstrate how punishment is politicized. First, we provide a contemporary foundation (demographics) of the correctional population i.e. jails, prisons, probation and parole. Second, a rationale is offered which explains why politicians are involved in the punishment of offenders. Third, is an examination of the manifestations of political punishment, i.e. war on drugs, mandatory minimum, three strikes laws and truth in sentencing. Ultimately, this chapter concludes that our correctional system is in dire straits.

Correctional Characteristics

Tables 7-1 through 7-5 and Figures 7-1 and 7-2 represent a concise picture of groups currently incarcerated._ Overall, we incarcerate a greater proportion of non-whites. Part of this phenomenon is attributable to the War on Drugs, uneven punishments of some drug offenders, and the economic reality of middle and lower class drug usage.

---

[7] Since the 1970s there has been a substantial sentencing reform movement. To begin, is the debate over indeterminate v. determinate sentencing. Indeterminate allows judges to set minimum and maximum terms of imprisonment. When an inmate reaches the minimum, he/she is eligible for parole. Often, the parole board will decide to grant early release (parole). Determinate takes away discretion of a judge. The sentence is prescribed by the sentencing authority and can not be deviated from by the judge. In addition, we have mandatory minimum, three strikes, sentencing guidelines and truth in sentencing.

Table 7-1: Total Inmates in Custody: Federal, State and Jail.

Year	Total Inmates in Custody	Prisoners in Custody Federal	State	Jail
1995	1,585,586	89,538	989,004	507,044
2000	1,935,919	133,921	1,176,269	621,149
2001	1,961,247	143,337	1,180,155	631,240
2002	2,033,022	151,618	1,209,331	665,475
2003	2,082,728	161,673	1,224,652	691,301
2004	2,131,180	169,370	1,241,034	713,990

Source: Paige Harrison & Allen Beck (April, 2005). Prison and Jail Inmates at Midyear 2004. Bureau of Justice Statistics. U.S. Department of Justice.

As the above demonstrates, since 1995, the population of inmates in federal prison has increased 7.8 %, followed by jails at 4.1% and states at 2.7%. To illustrate the correctional population since 1980, please see Figure 7-1.

Figure 7-1: Adult Correctional Populations: 1980-2003

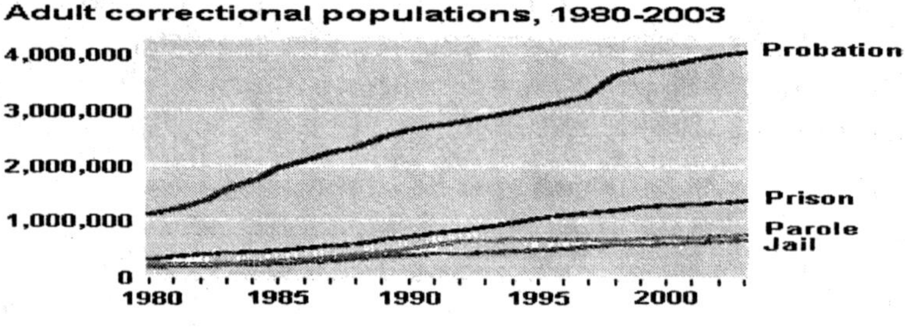

Source: www.ojp.usdoj.gov.

Table 7-2: Number of Inmates in State or Federal Prisons and Jails by Gender, Race and Age

	Male				Female			
Age	Total	White	Black	Hispanic	Total	White	Black	Hispanic
18-19	73,200	24,300	33,000	13,600	4,500	1,800	1,500	1,000
20-24	352,000	107,300	161,900	74,500	26,900	12,000	9,100	5,200
25-29	339,600	97,700	155,600	78,700	27,100	11,700	9,900	4,700
30-34	316,400	106,900	134,500	68,600	33,500	14,800	12,300	5,400
35-39	291,600	110,700	124,600	49,900	36,300	16,300	13,800	5,100
40-44	250,200	104,500	104,500	36,100	28,600	12,900	11,300	3,800
45-54	237,800	100,500	99,000	33,500	21,500	9,700	8,300	2,700
55-up	71,900	39,900	21,400	9,300	4,000	2,300	1,000	600

Source: Paige Harrison & Allen Beck (April, 2005). Prison and Jail Inmates at Midyear 2004._Bureau of Justice Statistics. U.S. Department of Justice.

Table 7-2 demonstrates that African American males are overrepresented compared to Caucasians and Hispanics. In fact, "an estimated 13% of black males in their late twenties were in jail or prison in 2004."[8] To demonstrate, the numbers of persons under probation and parole supervision, see Table 7-3.

[8] Paige Harrison & Allen Beck (April, 2005). Prison and Jail Inmates at Midyear 2004. Bureau of Justice Statistics. U.S. Department of Justice.

Table 7-3: Persons under Adult Community Correctional Supervision 1995-2003

Community Supervision		
Year	Probation	Parole
1995	3,077,861	679,421
2000	3,826,209	723,898
2001	3,931,731	732,333
2002	4,024,067	750,934
2003	4,073,987	774,588

Source: Lauren Glaze & Seri Palla (2004). Probation and Parole in the United States, 2003. Bureau of Justice Statistics. U.S. Department of Justice.

Table 7-4: Characteristics of Adults on Probation

	1995	2000	2003
Total	100%	100%	100%
Gender			
Male	79%	78%	77%
Female	21%	22%	23%
Race			
White	53%	54%	56%
Black	31%	31%	30%
Hispanic	14%	13%	12%
*Other	1%	2%	2%

*Other indicates American Indian/Alaska Native, Asian/Pacific Islander.

Source: Lauren Glaze & Seri Palla (2004). Probation and Parole in the United States, 2003. Bureau of Justice Statistics. U.S. Department of Justice.

Table 7-5: Characteristics of Adults on Parole

	1995	2000	2003
Total	100%	100%	100%
Gender			
Male	90%	88%	87%
Female	10%	12%	13%
Race			
White	34%	38%	40%
Black	45%	40%	41%
Hispanic	21%	21%	18%
*Other	1%	1%	2%

*Other indicates American Indian/Alaska Native, Asian/Pacific Islander.
Source: Lauren Glaze & Seri Palla (2004). Probation and Parole in the United States, 2003. Bureau of Justice Statistics. U.S. DOJ.

Politics of Punishment

As demonstrated, the correctional population is increasing at a substantial pace (see Figure 7-2). When considering inmates in the federal and state system, plus jails coupled with probation and parole, the number is approaching seven million individuals. To restate, "roughly 3.2% of the U.S. adult population, or one in every 32 adults" is under some form of custody.[9] To complicate the matter, "crime rates are approximately 20% lower today than they were in 1980. In fact, crime rates are at their lowest level in 20 years. But the number of people on probation is up almost 300% since 1980, the nation's prison population has increased by more than 400%, and the number of persons on parole has increased by almost the same proportion."[10] Ultimately, to understand this

---

[9] Lauren Glaze & Seripalla (2004). Probation and Parole in the United States, 2003. Bureau of Justice Statistics. U.S. Department of Justice.
[10] See Supra note 2. at p.4.

phenomenon, society must understand that the growth of the prison population is due to the fact that "policy makers decided to increase prison populations."[11] The question is why?

Figure 7-2: Incarceration Rate: 1980-2003

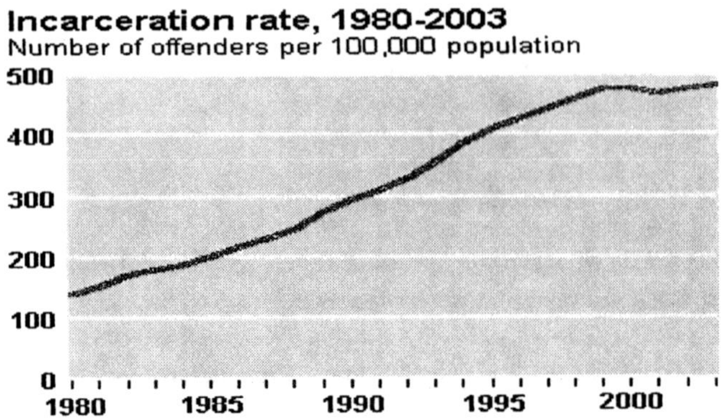

Source: www.ojp.usdoj.gov

Political Convenience

Politics and crime have an extensive and tumultuous history. This symbiotic relationship is responsible for the election of many politicians. According to Feldman, Schiraldi and Ziedenberg (2001), "Barry Goldwater was the first to campaign on crime control in an attempt to counter the prevailing liberal mood of the 1960's. Following Goldwater's lead was Richard Nixon who called for an increase in punitive crime control measures. This was followed by the Republican National Committee's unleashing of the now famous "Willie

---

[11] John Samaha (2006). Criminal Justice. p. 444. Thomson: Wadsworth. Belmont, CA.

Horton" advertisement during the race between Vice President George Bush and Massachusetts Governor Michael Dukakis."[12] It should be noted that politics is considered an unscrupulous business characterized by smiling faces and backroom deals. As the above demonstrates, politicians have been using the issue of crime as a campaign pledge/slogan for years. Why shouldn't they? The issue of crime is something in which all Americans have an opinion. To demonstrate, according to a recent public opinion poll, "Roughly four in ten Americans describe the problem of crime in the United States as either extremely (13%) or very serious (29%). This is down from 54% in 2003 and from 60% in 2000."[13] Concerning the public's opinion, what source of information or evidence do people base their opinion? Could it be television or print media which have sensationalized crime for over twenty years? Concerning the dissemination of fear, according to Chiricos (2004), "The United States has experienced two major moral panics (violence and drugs) since the mid 1980's"[14] that has created fear amongst citizens. Interestingly, as the public experiences fear, pressure is placed on politicians to search for a panacea. The ultimate sin lies in the fact that politicians (knowing the crime rate is down) are using the public's fear to justify their election or re-election and broaden the powers of the state and federal government. Manifestations

---

[12] Lisa Feldman, Vincent Schiraldi & Jason Ziedenberg. (2001) Too Little Too Late: President Clinton's Prison Legacy. Washington DC: The Justice Policy Institute.

[13] The Gallup Organization (March 15, 2005). American Public Opinion about Crime in the United States.

[14] Ted Chiricos (2004). The Media, Moral Panics and the Politics of Crime Control. pp. 41-61. In George Cole, Mark Gertz and Amy Bunger (2004). The Criminal Justice System: Politics and Policies. Thomson: Wadsworth. Belmont, CA.

of this fear include the "war on drugs," truth in sentencing, mandatory minimum laws and three strike laws.

War on Drugs

The crusades against the "war on drugs" have been a recurring theme of American politics since the late 1800's. According to Clear and Dammer (2003), "the latest manifestation began in 1982 when President Reagan declared his "war on drugs" and asked Congress to set aside more money for drug enforcement personnel and for prison space."[15] Subsequently, in 1986, President Reagan signed the Anti-Drug Abuse Act. This act provided $1.7 billion to fight the so called drug crisis and $97 million for the construction of new prisons. An additional $441 million was allocated for drug education and treatment. This act also created a mandatory sentencing law for drug-related offenses. In theory, the act was designed to achieve equal sentencing across the country and serve as a deterrent and punishment; however, this did not occur. Along with President Regan and his "war on drugs" rhetoric, was Mrs. Regan's "Just Say No Campaign." Along with a degree of naiveté Mrs. Regan appeared in television advertisements and crossed the country making personal appearances attempting to discourage children from using drugs. Interestingly, who was the target audience? According to Frontline, "Nancy Reagan's "Just Say No" focused on white, middle class children."[16] Following the Reagan's crusade was President Bush and his creation of the White House Office of National Drug Control Policy (ONDCP) in 1988. The purpose of this office is to develop policies, priorities, and objectives for the Nation's drug control program. As for goals, the office is

---

[15] See Supra note 6 at p. 50.

[16] Pbs.com. Frontline: Drug Wars.

tasked with: reducing illicit drug use, manufacturing, trafficking, and drug-related crime and violence. Ultimately, "the war on drugs has succeeded on one front by packing the Nation's prisons with drug offenders. However, many scholars believe that is about all it has achieved. Research on the impact of the war on drugs has shown little impact on the level of drug use or the crime rate."[17] According to Jensen, Gerber and Mosher (2004), "between 1980 and 2001, the number of persons in state and federal prisons for drug offenses increased by approximately 1,300%."[18]

Currently, 54% of those inmates in federal prison are there for drug offenses[19] compared to 20% of state inmates.[20] Figure 7-3 illustrates drug arrests.

Figure 7-3: Drug Arrests 1970-2003

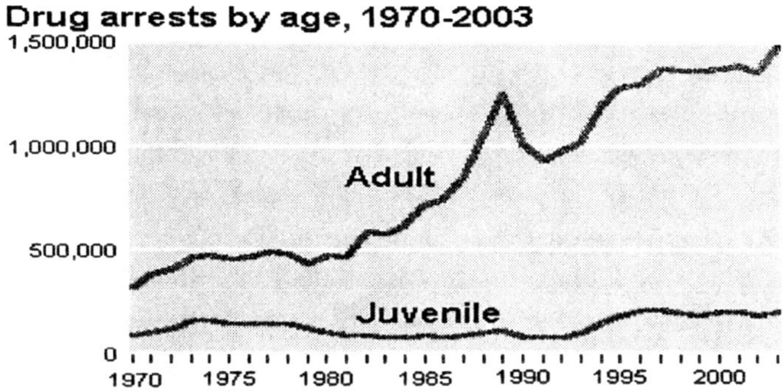

Source: www.ojp.usdoj.gov

---

[17] See Supra note 6 at p. 50.

[18] Eric Jensen, Jurg Gerber & Clayton Mosher (2004). Social Consequences of the War on Drugs: The Legacy of Failed Policy. Criminal Justice Policy Review, Vol. 15. no.1, pp.100-121.

[19] Thomas Bonczar & Tracy Snell (November, 2004). Capital Punishment, 2003. Bureau of Justice Statistics. U.S. Department of Justice.

[20] Paige Harrison & Allen Beck (2003). Prisoners in 2002. Bureau of Justice Statistics. U.S. Department of Justice.

As for the "war on drugs", who is the enemy? It appears politicians are at war with, "low level drug violators who are typically minority, poor and have few resources to defend themselves legally against ambitious law enforcement campaign."[21] What is the enemies' drug choice? It appears crack cocaine. According to Newsweek magazine:

- Crack ... is already creating social havoc in the ghettos of Los Angeles, New York and other large cities, and is rapidly spreading into the suburbs on both coasts.
- Crack has captured the ghetto and is inching its way into the suburbs.
- There are ominous signs that crack and rock dealers are expanding well beyond the inner cities.[22]

While recognizing the enemy and drug choice, politicians i.e. Congress in the 1980's decided to establish different penalties for crack and powder cocaine. The majority of politicians believed there was more harm associated with crack than with powder cocaine. Ultimately, a defendant convicted of selling 500 grams of powder cocaine or five grams of crack receives a five-year sentence. Moreover, a conviction of five kilos of powder cocaine and 50 grams of crack warrants a penalty of 10 years.[23] The difference in powder and crack penalties is often referred to as the 100:1 ratio between the drugs. To demonstrate the disparity in the correctional institutions, in 2001, there were 139,700 African

---

[21] Michael Welch (2005). Ironies of Imprisonment. p. 49. Sage Publications. Thousand Oaks, CA.
[22] Newsweek. March, 1986. Kids and Cocaine. pp. 58-65. Ted Chirocos (2004). The Media, Moral Panics and the Politics of Crime Control. pp. 41-61. In George Cole, Marcg Gertz and Amy Bunger (2004). The Criminal Justice System: Politics and Policies. Thomson: Wadsworth. Belmont, CA.
[23] Families Against Mandatory Minimums. famm.org.

Americans incarcerated for drug offenses compared to 57,300 Caucasians.[24] Ironically, a study published by the Journal of American Medical Association (JAMA) concluded that the physiological and psychoactive effects of cocaine are similar regardless of its form (powder or crack).[25]

Truth in Sentencing

Over the last thirty years, sentencing requirements and release policies have become very restrictive. Prevailing wisdom suggests that if a prisoner receives a ten or twenty year sentence in prison, he or she should "do the time." This attitude was shared by political leaders and the general public.[26] Subsequently, in 1994, U.S. Congress passed the Violent Crime Control and Law Enforcement Act.[27] This act provided incentives (money) to states who adopted "truth in sentencing" laws.[28] To comply with the Act, the state had to require an inmate to serve 85% of his or her sentence.[29] Obviously, as a result of this Act, is a correctional explosion. Currently, "forty states have instituted some form of truth in sentencing laws, though the future of such statutes is in doubt

---

[24] Paige Harrison & Allen Beck (July, 2003). Prisoners in 2002. Bureau of Justice Statistics. U.S. Department of Justice.

[25] Dorothy K. Hatsukami & Marian W. Fischman (November, 26, 1996). Journal of the American Medical Association. Crack Cocaine and Cocaine Hydrochloride: Are the Differences Myth or Reality?

[26] In the 1970's inmates were being released from prison after serving a short period of time; the sentence averaged 44 months.

[27] Paula Ditton & Doris Wilson (1999). Truth in Sentencing in State Prisons. Bureau of Justice Statistics. U.S. Department of Justice.

[28] Allen Beck & Lawrence Greenfield (1995). Violent Offenders in State Prisons: Sentences and Time Served. Bureau of Justice Statistics. U.S. Department of justice.

[29] See Supra note 6.

due to numerous challenges on constitutional grounds and the pressure of overflowing prisons."[30]

Mandatory Minimum Sentences

Beginning in the 1980's, mandatory minimum laws were designed to convey a no nonsense message by politicians. Ultimately, "by 1994, all fifty states had enacted at least one or more mandatory minimum sentencing law(s), and Congress had enacted numerous mandatory sentencing laws for federal offenders."[31] It is important to note that these laws remove sentencing discretion of judicial authorities. Most mandatory sentencing laws deal with either weapons or drug offenses; an example of a drug offense is selling drugs to a child within 1,000 feet of a school. As for the rationale of these laws:

- Equality: similar offense warrants similar sentence.
- Certainty: the public as well as the offenders know what to expect. If you do the crime, you will do the time.
- Just deserts: violent criminals and drug offenders, habitual offenders and criminals who use guns to commit crimes "deserve" to be incarcerated for lengthy time periods.
- Deterrence: sends a message that deters would-be offenders.
- Incapacitation: if offender is locked up, he or she can not inflict harm.[32]

---

[30] Larry Gaines & Roger Leroy Miller (2006). Criminal Justice in Action: The Core. pp. 260-261. Thomson: Wadsworth. Belmont, CA.
[31] See Supra note 6 at pp. 95-96.
[32] See Supra note 11 at p. 372.

The ultimate question is the validity of mandatory minimums. According to Samaha (2006), "evaluations suggest that mandatory minimum penalties in practice don't live up to their rationales or promises."[33] Moreover, according to the results from three independent firearm studies, mandatory minimums do not meet expectations.[34]

Three-Strike Laws (Habitual Offender Statute)

- On October 1, 1993, a twelve year old girl from California was at home with two friends having a slumber party. A mysterious man broke into her home, and forced her and the other girls to lie down. He threatened to cut their throats if they spoke. The man selected his victim, and told the other girls to count to one thousand. Ultimately, the little girl was raped and strangled to death. Her name was Polly Klass; the perpetrator was Richard Davis; a drifter with a lengthy violent criminal record.[35]

---

[33] Id p. 373.

[34] Colin Loftin, Milton Humann & David McDowell (1983). "Mandatory Sentencing and Firearms Violence: Evaluating an Alternative to Gun Control. Law and Society Review, Vol.17, pp.287-318. Colin Loftin & David McDowell (1984). The Deterrent Effects of the Florida Felony Firearm Rule. Journal of Law and Criminology, Vol.75, pp.250-259. David McDowell, Colin Loftin & Brian Wiersema (1992). A Comparative Study of Preventive Effects of Mandatory Sentencing Laws for Gun Crimes. Journal of Criminal Law and Criminology, Vol. 83, No.2 pp.378-394.

[35] Courttv.com.

This event served as the stimuli for the passage of three-strikes laws in California in 1994 (72% to 28%). These statutes require a person convicted of three felonies to serve a substantial prison sentence. Currently, twenty-six states and the federal government utilize three-strike statutes.[36] According to Clear and Dammer (2003), "the first implementation of three strike legislation was passed in the state of Washington in 1993."[37] Interestingly, individuals who advocate for three-strike laws maintain that such laws would deter people from committing crimes whereas, opponents recognize there may be some deterrent effect but ultimately, the prison population would explode. As for the state with the toughest three strike-laws… California leads the country. According to Vandiver (2005), "anyone in California who has been found guilty of three serious felonies would receive a sentence of no less than 25 years and no longer than a life sentence. While the first two felonies must be a serious felony, the third can be any felony."[38] It is important to note that the controversy surrounding California's three strike laws is monumental. There are many citizens who maintain that the laws are discriminatory and administered in an arbitrary manor, which violates the Eighth Amendment's cruel and unusual clause. As a result, in (2004), Proposition 66 was proposed to amend California's three-strikes law (Proposition 184), however, the proposition was defeated (53% to 47%).[39] Ultimately, the question remains do the three-strike laws work? Since the law passed, 42,000 individuals are serving time under California's three-strikes, which is close to all

[36] See Supra note 2.
[37] See Supra note 6 at p. 11.
[38] Donna Vandiver (2005). California, Texas, and California: The Big Three in Corrections. In Roslyn Muraskin (2005). Key Correctional Issues. Pearson: Prentice Hall. Upper Saddle River, NJ.
[39] Cnn.com.

states combined. However, out of the 42,000 inmates, are they all violent? Statistics indicate no.[40] According to Welch (2005),"The National Institute of Justice (NIJ) found that even though three-strike laws were intended to target serious offenders, more than 70% of defendants charged under such statutes were nonviolent offenders."[41] The following example is typical:

- In November of 1995, Leandro Andrade (on two separate occasions) attempted to steal videos estimated to cost $153.54 at K-mart. The nine videos (Christmas gifts) included such movies as *Snow White, Cinderella* and *Free Willie 2*. His sentence was fifty years. The United States Supreme Court in a 5-4 decision upheld the California's three-strike law.[42]

The Correctional Quandary

The correctional component of the criminal justice system is in dire straits. Over the last thirty-five years, politicians have waged a "war on drugs" created truth in sentencing, mandatory minimums and three--strike laws which by most accounts are considered failures. However, politicians are still engaged in politicizing punishment. Drawing on the fears of the public, politicians have created a quandary with no foreseeable outcome. It is important for politicians, as well as criminal justice practitioners, to realize that there are no panaceas. Rectifying the problem is no simple task. Two consequences of the politician's overzealousness with regards

---

[40] California Proposition 66: Limitations on Three Strikes Law. Sex, Crimes, Punishment and Initiative Statute.
[41] See Supra note 21.
[42] 123 S.Ct 1166 (2003).

to corrections are overcrowding and privatization. Concerning the overcrowding issue, according to Harrison and Beck (2004), the federal prisons are operating 39% over capacity, twenty states are operating between 90%-99% occupancy, 22 states are exceeding 100% occupancy, and the remaining seven are operating between 73%-88%.[43] To further demonstrate the overcrowding crisis, the Alabama prison system is designed to house 14,000 inmates; however, they collectively hold 27,885 inmates.[44] As for monies spent on inmates, Alabama spends $26 per day to incarcerate a prisoner, whereas the national average is $62 per inmate.[45] Alabama ranks last in the country in spending on medical care per inmate. The state spends approximately $5.50 per inmate, whereas the national average is $7.38.[46]

Another repercussion of politicized punishment is the use of private prisons (privatization). At midyear 2004 private prisons held 98,791 state and federal inmates. Overall, private prisons held 5.6% of all state inmates and 13.7% of all federal prisoners. Interestingly, out of the 98,791 state inmates, the south accounts for 47,706. These companies offer small scale and full scale services. While state and federal correctional administrators use private prisons to reduce overcrowding, lower operating expenses, and to avoid lawsuits, the companies are concerned with making money. Given this, is it possible that inmates will suffer at the expense of making a

---

[43] Paige Harrison & Allen beck (November, 2004). Prisoners in 2003. Bureau of Justice Statistics. U.S. Department of Justice. The state of Connecticut did not report prison capacities.
[44] Alabama Department of Corrections (July, 2005). Monthly Statistical Report.
[45] Equal Justice Initiative of Alabama. (March, 2005). Criminal Justice Reform in Alabama: A Report an Analysis of Criminal Justice Issues in Alabama.
[46] Id.

profit? For example, could educational, vocational, medical, food, mental health, recreation and rehabilitative services suffer at the expense of profits or the bottom line? Ultimately, is it the responsibility of a private company to administer punishment? Currently, politicians have undertaken another crusade; this involves sex offenders. On July 28th, 2005, without opposition, the United States Senate approved a measure that requires the creation of a national sex offender registry. Moreover, states and cities would have to maintain i.e. track these offenders when they are released from prison. Ultimately, how to deal with sex offenders in the United States is still undecided. However, if headlines are an indication, trouble is approaching: "Sex Offender Panic continues in Alabama".

Summary

Fear is a powerful emotion. Politicians, past and present, manipulate the American public to further ideological agendas. Examples include "the war on drugs", truth in sentencing, mandatory minimums, and three-strike laws. In addition, the direct consequences of these movements are prison overcrowding and the use of private prisons (privatization). Regrettably, politicians use criminal justice issues to further their campaign agendas. To avoid unnecessary laws and the infringement of the government, citizens should stay versed on agendas as well as the facts.

Chapter Eight   Capital Punishment

Is it possible that a sentence of death is too good for some convicted criminals? Should we as a society engage in some degree of humanity and spare those persons who commit such atrocious crimes? As a juror, what would be your initial reaction to the following criminal cases. In March of (2005), Jessica Marie Lunsford, a 9-year-old girl from Florida, was kidnapped from her bedroom. Her body was discovered days later near her parent's home. According to a medical examiner, evidence suggests that Jessica was sexually assaulted. The suspect, John Couey, who subsequently has a lengthy criminal history, allegedly confessed to abducting and killing Jessica and burying her in the yard of his half-sister's house, not far from the Lunsford's home[1].

Another case that has gained considerable public attention is the December (2002) murder of Laci Peterson and her unborn child Connor. During the trial, prosecutors maintained that her husband Scott killed Laci, a 27-year-old substitute teacher who was about a month away from delivering their first child. The District Attorney alleged that Scott dumped her body in the ocean and then told her family and police detectives that she had vanished from their home. Scott Peterson told detectives that he had last seen his wife on December 24, 2002, at approximately 9:30 a.m. when he left their home in the La Loma neighborhood of Modesto for a solo fishing trip in Berkeley, about an hour and a half drive away. Importantly, on April 13, 2003, the body of a full-term baby washed up on the shore of San Francisco Bay. The next day, a dog walker found the badly decomposed body of a woman. The area where the bodies were discovered was approximately three miles from the marina where Scott

---

[1] Fox News. March 21, 2005

Peterson claimed he was fishing. In November (2003) a jury of six women and six males found Peterson guilty of one count of first-degree murder and one count of second-degree murder of a fetus.[2]

As the above examples demonstrate, individuals have the ability to engage in actions that are beyond comprehension. What we as a society must decide is how to best deal with those who have committed crimes that shock the conscious. The focus of this chapter is to examine the state of capital punishment in the United States. This is accomplished through examining United States Supreme Court decisions, and modern political issues.

Current State of Capital Punishment

As a contemporary sentence, capital punishment is the harshest punishment a person can receive. From a historical perspective, "capital punishment was once common and imposed for crimes such as murder, rape, stealing, witchcraft, piracy, desertion, sodomy, adultery, concealing the birth or death of an infant, aiding runaway slaves, counterfeiting and forgery."[3] At present, there is no uniformity among the states regarding the usage, implementation and definition of a capital offense or crime. As of June 30, 2005, thirty-eight states, the United States Government, and the United States Military have crimes that are punishable by death.[4] Concerning definitional inconsistencies among the states, in Georgia; murder, kidnapping with bodily injury or ransom when the victim dies, aircraft hijacking or treason are punishable by

---

[2] CNN News. December 14, 2004.

[3] Frank Schmalleger & John Smykla (2005). Corrections in the Twenty-First Century. McGraw Hill: New York: New York

[4] Death Penalty Information Center: Facts about the Death penalty (June 30, 2005).

death.[5] In California, first degree murder with special circumstances, train wrecking, treason, and perjury causing extortion warrant the death penalty. In Louisiana, first degree murder; aggravated rape of a victim under the age of 12 and treason are capital crimes.[6] It is Important to recognize that while the United States Constitution does not discuss the death penalty, in "1790 the first Congress mandated the death penalty for several offenses including treason, willful murder on federal property, forgery, piracy, counterfeiting, and several crimes on the high seas."[7] Currently, federal laws provide for the death penalty in both homicide and non-homicide crimes.[8]

Without hesitation, the number of federal death penalty crimes is a product of politics. Specifically, President Reagan's Anti-Drug Abuse Act, President Clinton's Violent Crime Control and Law Enforcement Act and the USA PATRIOT ACT of 2001 contribute to the number of federal

---

[5] Bureau of Justice Statistics: Capital Punishment 2003.

[6] Id.

[7] See Supra note 3 at p. 540.

[8] Homicide related crimes include genocide, mailing of injurious articles with intent to kill or injure resulting in death, murder by the use of a weapon of mass destruction, murder for hire, murder of a court officer or juror, murder committed by the use of a firearm during a crime of violence or a drug related trafficking crime, murder related to sexual exploitation of children, willful wrecking of a train resulting in death, murder involving torture, murder during a kidnapping, murder of a foreign official, murder during a hostage taking, murder related to the smuggling of aliens, destruction of aircraft, motor vehicles, or related facilities resulting in death, civil rights offenses resulting in death, assassination or kidnapping resulting in the death of the President or Vice President and murder of a federal judge or law enforcement officer.
Non-homicide crimes include espionage, treason, trafficking in large quantities of drugs or attempting, authorizing or advising the killing of any officer, juror or witness in cases involving a continuing criminal enterprise regardless of whether such killing actually occurs.

capital offenses.[9]

Contemporary Death Row Characteristics

As of June 30, 2005, there have been 972 executions since 1976. As figure 8-1 illustrates, executions reached their highest point in 1999 with 98 individuals. There have been a modest 28 at the midpoint of 2005.

Figure 8-1: Number of Executions Since 1976

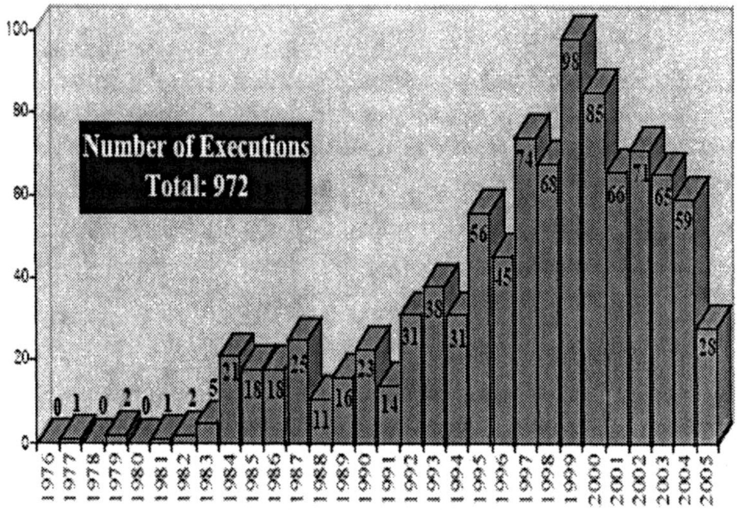

Source: Death Penalty Information Center: Facts about the Death Penalty. June 30, 2005.

As for the race of those executed, 58% are Caucasian, 34%

[9] Anti-Drug Abuse Act 1988 (drug trafficking), Violent Crime Control and Law Enforcement Act 1994 (terrorist homicides, murder of a Federal law enforcement officer, large-scale drug trafficking, drive-by-shootings and carjacking resulting in death). USA PATRIOT ACT 2001 (Terrorism).

African American, 6% Hispanic, and 2% other. The gender of those executed is approximately 99% male. When considering the race of the victim in death penalty cases, "over 80% of the murder victims in cases resulting in an execution were white, even though nationally only 50% of the murder victims are generally white."[10] See Table 8-1 for a defendant/victim racial breakdown.

Table 8-1: Defendant-Victim Relationship

Defendant-victim racial combinations

	White Victim	Black Victim	Latino/a Victim	Asian Victim	Native American Victim
White Defendant	522 (54.60%)	12 (1.26%)	8 (.84%)	3 (.31%)	0 (0%)
Black Defendant	199 (20.82%)	99 (10.36%)	12 (1.26%)	7 (.73%)	0 (0%)
Latino/a	30 (3.14%)	2 (.21%)	24 (2.51%)	1 (.10%)	0 (0%)
Asian Defendant	2 (.21%)	0 (0%)	0 (0%)	5 (.52%)	0 (0%)
Native Amer. Def.ican	12 (1.26%)	0 (0%)	0 (0%)	0 (0%)	2 (.21%)
TOTAL:	765 (80.02%)	113 (11.82%)	44 (4.60%)	16 (1.67%)	2 (.21%)

Note: *In addition, there were 16 defendants executed for the murders of multiple victims of different races. Of those, 9 defendants were white, 4 black and 3 Latino. (1.67%)*

Source: NAACP Legal Defense and Educational Fund, Inc. Death Row U.S.A. April 1, 2005.

According to the NCAAP criminal justice project, there, are 3,452 death row inmates. Table 8-2 gives a state by state breakdown. As evident, California, Texas and Florida have the largest death row population. Interestingly, in the correctional literature these states are often referred to as the "big three."

[10] Death Penalty Information Center: Facts about the Death Penalty (June 30, 2005).

At midyear 2004, these states housed a collective total 419,886 inmates.[11]

Table 8-2: Death Row Inmates by State.

California	644	S. Carolina	77	Utah	10
Texas	441	Mississippi	70	Illinois	10
Florida	384	Missouri	56	Maryland	9
Pennsylvania	230	Arkansas	38	Connecticut	9
Ohio	198	Kentucky	37	Nebraska	9
N. Carolina	197	U.S. Gov't	36	U.S. Military	7
Alabama	195	Indiana	33	Kansas	7
Arizona	129	Oregon	32	Montana	4
Georgia	112	Virginia	23	S. Dakota	4
Tennessee	107	Idaho	22	Colorado	3
Oklahoma	98	Delaware	19	New York	3
Louisiana	91	New Jersey	15	New Mexico	2
Nevada	86	Washington	11	Wyoming	2

Source: Death Row USA. April 1, 2005.

As for racial composition, of the 3,452 inmates sentenced to death, 42% (1,440) are African American, 10% (359) are Hispanic, 46% (1,572) are Caucasian, and 2% (81) are Native American, Asian or Unknown. As for gender, 98% (3,399) are male. The education of death row inmates is of some concern. Approximately 52% of those convicted failed to graduate from high school. Approximately 38% of the inmates are high school graduates or GED recipients. Only 9% have completed

[11] Texas 169,110, California 166, 053 and Florida 84, 733. Paige Harrison & Allen Beck. (April, 2005). Prison and Jail Inmates at Midyear 2004. Bureau of Justice Statistics.

some college.[12] With respect to marital status, 23% of the prisoners are married, 21% are divorced or separated, 3% are widowed and 54% have never been married.[13] With respect to the number of executions by state, we could possibly assume that Texas, California or Florida executes at a higher rate than other states. This is not necessarily the case.

Table 8-3: Number of Executions by State Since 1976

	Total	'04	'05		Total	'04	'05
Texas	345	23	9	Nevada	11	2	0
Virginia	94	5	0	Mississippi	6	0	0
Oklahoma	77	6	2	Utah	6	0	0
Missouri	64	0	3	Maryland	4	1	0
Florida	60	2	1	Washington	4	0	0
Georgia	38	2	2	Nebraska	3	0	0
N. Carolina	36	4	2	Pennsylvania	3	0	0
S. Carolina	33	4	1	Kentucky	2	0	0
Alabama	32	2	2	Montana	2	0	0
Louisiana	27	0	0	Oregon	2	0	0
Arkansas	26	1	0	Colorado	1	0	0
Arizona	22	0	0	Connecticut	1	0	1
Ohio	16	7	1	Idaho	1	0	0
Delaware	13	0	0	New Mexico	1	0	0
Indiana	14	0	3	Tennessee	1	0	0
Illinois	12	0	0	Wyoming	1	0	0
California	11	0	1	U.S.Gov't	3	0	0

Source: DPIC: Facts about the Death Penalty (June 30, 2005).

[12] Death Row U.S.A. April 1, 2005
[13] Thomas Bronczar & Tracy Snell (November, 2004) Capital Punishment 2003. Bureau of Justice Statistics. U.S. Department of Justice.

As Table 8-3 indicates, Florida, Texas and California account for approximately 43% of those executed. Something to question is the actual murder rate in these respective states. According to Table 8-4, the murder rate for these states is by all accounts relatively low. By comparison, the national murder rate for 2003 is 5.7 compared to 9.8 in 1991. As you can see, murder is on a decrease just as overall violent crime in the United States. In 1991, there were 252,153,092 persons living in the United States. The number of violent crimes reported totaled 1,911,767. In comparison, by year end 2003, the population totaled 290,809,777, whereas the number of violent crimes was 1,381,259. Further, according to the UCR, the overall murder rate has decreased 29.3% since 1994.[14] In addition, the number of murders decreased from 23,326 to 16,503 in 1994 and 2003 respectively.

Table: 8- 4 UCR Murder Rates 2003: California, Florida and Texas

State	Year	Murder Rate
California	2003	6.8
Florida	2003	5.5
Texas	2003	5.9

Source: UCR Crime in the United States 2003.

Another interesting statistic is execution by region. Figure 8-2 demonstrates that the South is leading all other regions by a substantial margin.

[14] Uniform Crime Report (2003).

Figure 8-2: Executions by Region

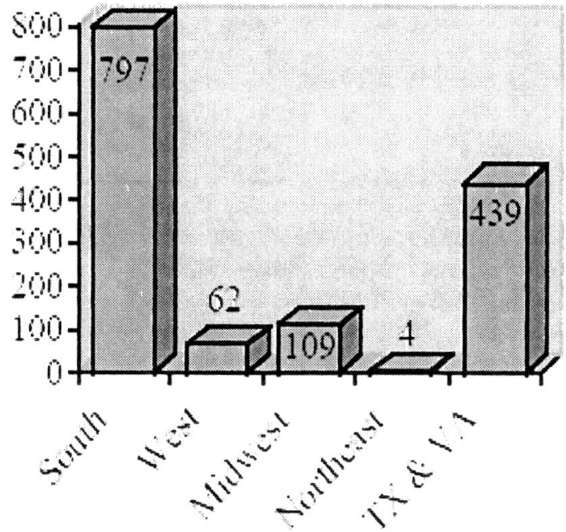

*Federal executions are listed in the region in which the crime was committed.

Source: DPIC: Facts about the Death Penalty (June 30, 2005)

Is there a relationship between the numbers of executions by region and murder rates? We established earlier that California, Texas and Florida have relatively low murder rates, while ultimately accounting for 43% of those executed. Geographically, the UCR considers Florida and Texas as southern states, whereas California is categorized as a western state. According to the UCR, the South has the highest murder rate. Interestingly, "the South accounts for over 80% of executions. The Northeast which has less than 1% of all executions again had the lowest murder rates."[15] (See Figure 8-3)

---

[15] See Supra note 10.

Figure 8-3: UCR 2003 Murder Rates Per 100,000

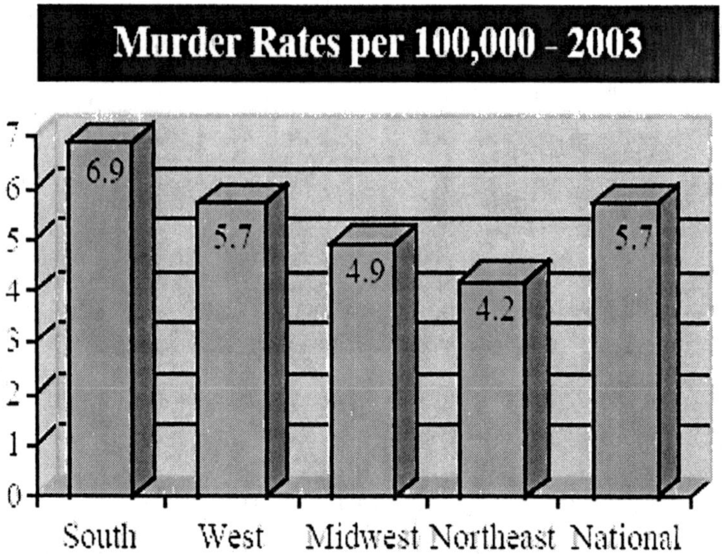

Source: DPIC: Facts about the Death Penalty (June 30, 2005).

Methods of Execution in the United States

Throughout the years, there have been many methods of execution. Examples include, "drawing and quartering, burning, and boiling a convict alive."[16] Currently, the United States prohibits the use of these punishments. Why? These punishments are considered too barbaric and inhumane. Contemporary methods of execution now include hanging, firing squad, lethal gas, lethal injection or electrocution.[17]

---

[16] Larry Gaines & Le Roy Miller (2006). Criminal Justice in Action: The Core. Wadsworth: Thomson: Belmont; CA. p.271.

[17] Thomas Bronczar & Tracy Snell (January, 2004). Capital Punishment 2003. Bureau of Justice Statistics. U.S. Department of Justice. Lethal

Death Row Conditions

Individuals who are under a sentence of death are segregated from the prison congregation. Until execution these inmates spend their days and nights living in a hell on earth environment termed death row. Persons sentenced to death are living a life marked by frustration, anger and reflection. This reflection far too often takes an inmate down a road that is marked by past episodes of violence, abuse of drugs and alcohol and disjointed relationships. In mainstream society, we far too often hear politicians use words such as deterrence, punishment and rehabilitation. For the death row inmate, rehabilitation is absent. Death row inmates spend approximately 23 hours of the day in their "five by eight or six by nine foot cell."[19] The architecture and design of death row

---

injection: Alabama, Arizona, Arkansas, California, Colorado, Connecticut, Delaware, Florida, Georgia, Idaho, Illinois, Indianan , Kansas, Kentucky, Louisiana, Maryland, Mississippi, Missouri, Montana, Nevada, New Hampshire, New Jersey, New Mexico, New York, North Carolina, Ohio, Oregon, Pennsylvania, South Carolina, Tennessee, Texas, Utah, Virginia, Washington, Wyoming. Electrocution: Alabama, Arkansas, Florida, Kentucky, Nebraska, Oklahoma, South Carolina, Tennessee, Virginia. Hanging: Delaware, New Hampshire, Washington. Lethal gas: Arizona, California, Missouri, Wyoming. Firing Squad: Idaho, Oklahoma and Utah. According to the Bureau of Justice Statistics, seventeen states authorized more than 1method -- lethal injection and an alternative method -- generally at the election of the condemned prisoner; however, 5 of these 17 stipulated which method must be used depending on the date of sentencing; 1 authorized hanging only if lethal injection could not be given; and if lethal injection is ever ruled to be unconstitutional, 1 authorized lethal gas, and 1 authorized electrocution or firing squad. The method of execution of Federal prisoners is lethal injection, pursuant to 28 CFR, Part 26. For offenses under the Violent Crime Control and Law Enforcement Act of 1994, the method is that of the state in which the conviction took place (18 U.S.C. 3596)" (p.4).

[19] Id. p.549.

is marked by steel and cement. Toilets and sinks are often made of metal, whereas beds are a slab of cement with a thin mattress on top. The rigidity and unbending nature of death row is in direct contrast to the inmate's former life. One can only imagine how an inmate copes as the days turn into months and the months turn into years. The chaotic nature of death row is characterized by "shouting, flushing toilets, opening and closing steel doors, janitorial work, the blaring of televisions, radios, and voices wailing."[20] While death row inmates are allowed non-contact visits, and some allow for conjugal visits, most of these inmates lose these personal contacts as time passes.

Contemporary Issues of Capital Punishment

Racial Bias

On October 12, 1978, an African American with the last name McCleskey was convicted of two counts of armed robbery and one count of murder in the Superior Court of Fulton County, Georgia. McCleskey's convictions resulted from the robbery of a furniture store and the killing of a Caucasian police officer during the course of the robbery. The jury during the penalty hearing considered the mitigating and aggravating circumstances of McClesky's conduct and recommended the death penalty on the murder charge. The trial court accepted the recommendation as did the Georgia Supreme Court. After years of seeking post-conviction relief in state courts, McClesky sought habeas corpus relief in Federal District Court. His petition suggested that the Georgia capital sentencing process was administered in a racially discriminatory manner in violation of the Eighth and

[20] See Supra note 18. p. 549.

Fourteenth Amendments. To offer support for his claim, McClesky offered a statistical study that demonstrates a disparity in the imposition of the death sentence in Georgia based on the murder victim's race and, to a lesser extent, the defendant's race.[21] The study is based on over 2,000 murder cases that occurred in Georgia during the 1970's. The data includes relationships such as victim's race, the defendant's race, and the various combinations of such persons' races. Further, the study suggests that African American defendants who killed Caucasian victims have a greater chance of being sentenced to death. In 1987, the United States Supreme Court assumed the validity of the Baldus study but found the statistics insufficient to demonstrate unconstitutional discrimination in the Fourteenth Amendment context or to show irrationality, arbitrariness, and capriciousness under the Eighth Amendment.[22] Since the McClesky case, the race of the defendant has been examined closely.[23] In 2000, Governor Parris Glendening of Maryland ordered a study investigating race and its role in the death penalty. The study was conducted by researchers at the University of Maryland. Results indicate that the state's death penalty system is tainted with racial bias and that geography plays a significant role in who faces a capital conviction. Ultimately, this study concludes that

---

[21] David Baldus, a statistician, was sought to conduct a statistical study of capital sentencing in Georgia. The data from the study indicated that those who killed Caucasians were ten times more likely to receive a death sentence than those who killed African-Americans. After accounting for nonracial variables, the study concluded that capital defendants found to be guilty of killing Caucasians were more than four times as likely to be sentenced to death as those found to be guilty of killing African-Americans.

[22] *McClesky v. Kemp* 481 U.S. 279. (1987).

[23] Adam Hines. Life or Death Mistakes: Cultural Stereotyping, Capital Punishment, and Regional Race-Based Trends in Exoneration and Wrongful Execution. 82.U. Det. Mercy L Review.181.

defendants are much more likely to be sentenced to death if they have killed a Caucasian person.[24] In (2001), a North Carolina study examined all homicide cases which occurred over a five year period (January 1, 1993 through December 31, 1997). Results indicate that the odds of receiving a death sentence rose by 3.5 times or more among those defendants (of whatever race) who murdered Caucasians.[25] When examining executions since 2003, forty-one African Americans have been executed in the United States. During this same period, only one Caucasian was executed for killing an African American and this case involved a Caucasian victim as well. Ironically, this case occurred in Texas, which has executed only one Caucasian out of 336 inmates since (1976). Today, African Americans account for 42% of death row inmates.[26] Compared to census data, African American death row inmates more than triple the African American population.[27]

Mental Deficiencies

The morning was cool on October 25, 1979, when Pamela Carpenter was brutally raped, beaten, and stabbed with a pair of scissors in her home in Livingston, Texas.[28] She eventually died a few hours later, however, before her passing she gave a description of her attacker. This description led sheriff's deputies to Johnny Paul Penry. Subsequently, after eleven hours of interrogation, he signed two statements confessing to

---

[24] Raymond Paternoster & Robert Brane (Jan. 2003). An Empirical Analysis of Maryland's Death Sentencing System With Respect To The Influence Of Race And Legal Jurisdiction.
[25] Jack Boger & Issac Unah (April 16, 2001). Race and The Death Penalty in North Carolina: An Empirical Analysis 1993-1997.
[26] See Supra note 12.
[27] Census 2000. Profile of General Demographics.
[28] 492 U.S. 302 (1989)

the crime and was charged with capital murder.[29] Penry was twenty-two years old at the time of the crime. According to a child psychologists, Penry has an IQ between 50 and 63, which indicates mild to moderate retardation. Moreover, Penry's social maturity, or ability to function in the world, was that of a nine or ten year old. The child psychologist also suggested that Penry had the mental age of a 6 1/2-year-old.[30] The United States Supreme Court rejected the premise that executing a mentally retarded man was cruel and unusual under the Eighth Amendment.[31] At the time of this ruling only two states had laws prohibiting the execution of the mentally retarded.[32] See Figure 8-4 for Penry's drawing.

Figure 8-4: Penry Drawing

At approximately midnight on August 16, 1996, Atkins and William Jones, armed with a semiautomatic handgun, abducted Eric Nesbitt.[33] Atkins and Jones proceeded to rob him of the money in his possession and then drove him to an

---

[29] Id.
[30] Id.
[31] Id.
[32] Maryland and Georgia.
[33] No. 00-8452.

automated teller machine in his pickup truck where cameras recorded their withdrawal of additional cash.[34] The two assailants eventually took Nesbitt to an isolated location where he was shot eight times and killed.[35] Daryl Atkins was convicted of abduction, armed robbery, and capital murder, and sentenced to death. Just as Johnny Paul Penry, Atkins was diagnosed with mental retardation. According to Dr. Evan Nelson, Atkins was mildly mentally retarded.[36] Nelson's conclusion "was based on interviews with people who knew Atkins, a review of school and court records and the administration of a standard intelligence test which indicated that Atkins had an IQ of 59."[37] The court held that the execution of a mentally retarded person is a violation of the Eighth Amendment's cruel and unusual punishment clause. An important question is, why does the United States Supreme Court involve itself in a matter it had recently ruled on? Further, What is the difference, if anything, between the Penry and Atkins' case? The answer is clearly politics. In the Penry decision, Justice O' Connor suggested no national consensus had developed against executing the mentally retarded. By comparison, in the Atkins opinion, Justice Stephens for the majority suggested a national consensus had developed against the execution of the mentally retarded.[38] This consensus was measured by the fact that "beginning in 1988 Arizona, Arkansas, Colorado, Connecticut, Florida, Georgia, Indiana, Kansas, Kentucky, Maryland, Missouri, Nebraska, New Mexico, New York, North Carolina, South Carolina, South Dakota, Tennessee, Washington and the federal government passed statutes banning the execution of

---

[34] Id.
[35] Id.
[36] Id.
[37] Id.
[38] Id.

the mentally retarded."[39]

With the discussion, we must recognize that the states, as well as the federal government each have their definition of what constitutes mental retardation. According to the American Association on Mental Retardation, "Mental retardation is a disability characterized by significant limitations both in intellectual functioning and in adaptive behavior as expressed in conceptual, social, and practical adaptive skills."[40] The limitation in intellect is measured by an intelligent quotient score of seventy (70) or below. This disability originates before age 18. An example of states' definitional differences is as follows, In Arkansas, mental retardation is measured by "significantly sub-average general intellectual functioning accompanied by significant deficits or impairments in adaptive functioning, and manifested in the developmental period. The age of onset is 18. There is a rebuttable presumption of mental retardation when the defendant has an IQ of 65 or below."[41] By comparison, Maryland defines a mentally retardated person as "an individual who has significantly sub-average intellectual functioning as evidenced by an IQ of 70 or below on an individually administered IQ test, and impairment in adaptive behavior. The age of onset is before the age of 22."[42]

<u>Juveniles</u>

An issue in the administration of justice is criminal culpability. Specifically, at what age does a child know right from wrong? Common law suggests children under the age of seven do not comprehend right from wrong. Between the age

---

[39] See Supra note 3.
[40] American Association of Mental Retardation: Fact Sheet. Aamr.org.
[41] Ark. Code. Ann. Sect-5-4-618.
[42] Md. Code. Ann.Art. 27 Sect. 412.

of eight and thirteen there is a rebuttable presumption. Lastly, from fourteen years of age and older, a child unquestionably knows right from wrong. By 1945, every state had developed a juvenile court system[43] based on the premise that, "children are not fully responsible for criminal conduct and are capable of being rehabilitated."[44] Moreover, the state has not only the right but a duty to care for children who are neglected, delinquent, or in some other way disadvantaged."[45] In the following case, decide whether a child or an adult committed the crime. On the morning of January 23, 1983, William Thompson actively participated in the brutal murder of his former brother-in-law.[46] Evidence showed that the victim had been shot twice, and his throat, chest, and abdomen had been cut. The victim had a broken leg and multiple bruises.[47] His body was chained to a concrete block and thrown into a river where it remained for approximately four weeks. William Thompson and three others were sentenced to death. At the time of the crime, Petitioner Thompson was fifteen years of age. In this case, Supreme Court justices Stevens, Brennan, Marshall and Blackmun "concluded that the 'cruel and unusual punishments' prohibition of the Eighth Amendment, made applicable to the States by the Fourteenth Amendment, prohibits the execution of a person who was under 16 years of age at the time of his or her offense."[48] Subsequently, in the following year, the Supreme Court upheld the sentence of death for Kevin Stanford who committed murder on January 7, 1981. At the time, Stanford was approximately 17 years and 4 months of age.[49] Stanford and an accomplice repeatedly

---

[43] See Supra note 16.
[44] Id p. 370.
[45] Id p. 369.
[46] 487 U.S. 815
[47] Id.
[48] Id.
[49] 492 U.S. 361 (1989).

raped and sodomized twenty year old Barbel Poore during and after their commission of a robbery at a gas station where she worked as an attendant.[50] Stanford then drove Ms. Poole to an isolated area in close proximity to the station and shot her pointblank in the face and then in the back of her head. A second case upheld by the Supreme Court involves a defendant who was sixteen years and six months at the time he committed murder. On July 27, 1985, Heath Wilkins planned to rob a convenience store and murder "whoever was behind the counter" because a dead person can't talk."[51] Ultimately, Wilkins stabbed Nancy Allen, a 26-year-old mother of two who was working behind the sales counter.[52] By the time Wilkins finished, Allen was stabbed more than eight times. Wilkins and an accomplice left Allen to die on the floor after helping themselves to liquor, cigarettes, rolling papers and approximately $450 in cash and checks.[53] In sum, the United States Supreme Court upheld the execution of those above the age of sixteen but not less than fifteen years of age.

Interestingly, the Supreme Court decided to hear another case involving a juvenile in October 13, 2004. Here, Christopher Simmons, age 17, a junior in high school, committed the murder of Shirley Cook after breaking and entering her home while she slept.[54] Simmons entered Mrs. Cook's bedroom, used duct tape to cover her eyes and mouth and bind her hands.[55] Mrs. Cook was carried to her minivan and driven to a state park. Cook was escorted to the Meramec River, where she was thrown from the bridge, eventually drowning in the water.[56] The United States Supreme Court on

---

[50] Id.
[51] Id.
[52] Id.
[53] Id.
[54] No. 03-633.
[55] Id.
[56] Id.

March 1, 2005, in a 5-4 vote held that the Eighth and Fourteenth Amendments, forbid the execution of offenders who were under the age of 18 when their crimes were committed.[57] Justice Kennedy, writing for the majority stated, "When a juvenile offender commits a heinous crime, the State can exact forfeiture of some of the most basic liberties, but the State cannot extinguish his life and his potential to attain a mature understanding of his own humanity."[58] Before this ruling and since 1976, twenty-two death row inmates had been executed for crimes they committed as juveniles.[59] Is it possible that a national consensus exists regarding the prohibition against executing those who commit crimes as juveniles? Did the justices follow the same logic as in Atkins? At the time, nineteen states and the federal government stipulated a minimum of at least eighteen years of age for capital punishment.[60] Coincidentally, as of April 15, 2005, there were seventy-two juveniles sentenced to death (all male).

Arbitrariness

Are death sentences reliable? In the United States, can we, with absolute certainty, assure ourselves that the convicted defendant is in fact guilty of the alleged crime? Does the courtroom workgroup make errors in the processing of cases? The arbitrariness of death sentences has continued to receive intense scrutiny in the United States. Unfortunately, the chances of a defendant in a capital case receiving a death sentence appears to depend on the quality of defense counsel

[57] Id.
[58] Id.
[59] Death Penalty Information Center (June 30, 2005).
[60] California, Colorado, Connecticut, Illinois, Indiana, Kansas, Maryland, Missouri, Montana, Nebraska, New Jersey, New Mexico, New York, Ohio, Oregon, South Dakota, Tennessee, Washington and Wyoming.

and the jurisdiction where the crime was committed.[61] A recent study by James Liebman (2001) suggests that the capital system is in dire straights. Liebman and associates investigated capital cases from 1973-1995.[62] The study revealed that of the 5,760 capital sentences and 4,578 appeals examined, a serious error undermined the reliability of these sentences. Specifically, the overall rate of prejudicial error in the American capital punishment system was 68%. In other words, "courts found serious reversible error in nearly seven out of every ten of the thousands of capital sentences that were fully reviewed during the period."[63] In addition, "capital trials produce so many mistakes it takes three judicial inspections to catch them leaving grave doubt as to whether or not we do catch them all."[64] To further put the concept of arbitrariness in perspective, "six states account for nearly two-thirds of all executions (Florida, Louisiana, Missouri, Oklahoma, Texas, and Virginia), while twelve states (Alaska, Hawaii, Iowa, Maine, Massachusetts, Michigan, Minnesota, North Dakota, Rhode Island, Vermont, West Virginia, Wisconsin and the District of Columbia) do not provide for capital punishment.

Innocence

In the United States, we should not operate under the assumption that the criminal justice system i.e. capital system is without error. The criminal justice system employs humans and errors will occur. Since (1976), there have been 121 exonerations of death row inmates.[66] These inmates were

---

[61] See Supra note 16.
[62] James Liebman (2001). A Broken System: Error rates in Capital Cases.
[63] Id. Executive Summary.
[64] Id. Executive Summary.

found guilty on such issues as false confession, prosecutorial misconduct, incompetent attorney, police misconduct, informants or snitches, faulty eyewitness testimony and mistaken identification. In (2000), former Illinois Republican Governor George Ryan declared a moratorium on all death row executions. The Governor was convinced that the system had produced so many errors it could not be trusted to determine life and death verdicts. One of the major stimuli for the moratorium was Anthony Porter. Porter spent sixteen years on death row for double murder. Two days before his execution he was found innocent and released. In Illinois, thirteen death row inmates have been exonerated since (1976). Given this, Governor Ryan, on January 11, 2003, a few days before his governorship expired, emptied death row, granting four pardons and 167 commutations for those with death sentences.[67] The Governor's actions were not an isolated event. Since this time, President Bush, in his February 2, 2005, state of the union discussed capital crimes. According to President Bush, "because one of the main sources of our national unity is our belief in equal justice, we need to make sure Americans of all races and backgrounds have confidence in the system that provides justice. In America we must make doubly sure no person is held accountable for a crime he or she did not commit. Consequently, we are dramatically expanding the use of DNA evidence to prevent wrongful conviction. Soon I will send to Congress a proposal to fund special training for defense counsel in capital cases, because people on trial for their lives must have competent lawyers by their side."[68] It is important to recognize that there is no sure method in determining how many of the 972 executed since (1976) may have been innocent. For the most part, the courts

---

66 Deathpeanltyinfo.org.

[67] See Supra note 65 at p. 277.

[68] President Bush (February 2, 2005) State of the Union Address.

do not hear claims of innocence when a defendant is deceased. Moreover, defense attorneys allocate their time to cases in which clients' lives can be saved.

Public Opinion

There exists no other criminal justice issue that garners as much attention as capital punishment. As a matter of fact, most persons will freely give their opinion concerning the matter at hand. One poll that has a lengthy history of investigating the death penalty is the Gallup poll. Since (1936), the Gallup poll has asked the following question to respondents: "Are you in favor of the death penalty for a person convicted of murder?" In (1936), 59% of respondents stated yes, whereas 38% were against.[69] The popularity of the death penalty has fluctuated over the years. In (1994), the death penalty achieved its highest level of acceptability at 80%. In contrast, the lowest level of support was in (1966) in which 42% were opposed.[70] A Gallup poll conducted between May 2-5, 2005 indicates 74% are in favor of the death penalty for a person convicted of murder.[71] As an option, the Gallup poll asked respondents: Which do you think is the better penalty for murder, the death penalty or life imprisonment with absolutely no possibility of parole? Interestingly, support for the death penalty declined to 56% and life imprisonment increased to 39%.[72] Without question, the death penalty is related to political ideology. According to a Gallup poll, those who are deemed conservative favor the death penalty 62% to 36% life imprisonment. In direct contrast, liberals favor the

---

[69] Gallup Poll News Service. May 19, 2003
[70] Id.
[71] Id.
[72] Id.

death penalty 37% to 60% life imprisonment.[73] A recent CBS News poll found the public split on the death penalty. When respondents were asked "What do you think should be the penalty for persons convicted of murder" the death penalty, life in prison with no chance of parole, or a long prison sentence with a chance of parole, 39% chose the death penalty, 39% chose life with no parole, 6% said a long sentence with parole, while 13% were unsure.[74] Another interesting factor that influences one's belief about the death penalty is educational attainment. Those individuals with postgraduate degrees prefer life imprisonment 62% compared to 37% for death.[75] Income is a third factor that helps us understand views toward the death penalty. Research suggests people with higher incomes are more likely to support capital punishment than people with lower incomes.[76] Why might this be the case? Is it possible that those economically sound have a distorted view of the criminal justice system? Specifically, they believe all defendants have access to due process (best attorneys, expert witnesses and jury consultants). Or is it possible that those with less income view the criminal justice system as corrupt and adversarial? Thus, life in prison without parole is more acceptable than death. Ask yourself whether we should heed the following advice; is it better that ten guilty person's escape than one innocent person suffer?[77]

Summary

The death penalty has an intriguing history. Twenty-first Century America is overwhelmingly punitive. However, there

---

[73] Id.
[74] CBS News. April 17, 2005.
[75] Gallup Poll News Service. May 19, 2003.
[76] See Supra note 3.
[77] William Blackstone.

are some mitigating circumstances. With the passage of time, the death penalty will lose its appeal. Death is certainly no deterrent to crime. Based on the number of those inmates exonerated from death row, society should not take a chance on executing an innocent person. Research demonstrates that racial bias is common and many death row inmates suffer from mental deficiencies. In addition, the process is arbitrary and public opinion while substantially high decreases when life without parole is an option. Is death too good for some? Which is worse, death or living twenty to forty years in a five by eight or six by nine cell? For those who are curious, obtain some masking tape and measure off the dimensions on a smooth floor (surface). Stand or sit for a few hours without breaking the parameter. There are some people who suggest incapacitating someone for twenty to forty years in this respect is cruel and unusual.

Chapter Nine Politics of Tort Reform

Powerful lobbies such as the Trial Lawyers Association, American Bar Association, American Medical Society, U.S. Chamber of Commerce, insurance companies, and both major political parties have waged aggressive campaigns over the issue of civil litigation. These parties disagree over one central question: is the United States a litigious society? Advocates of tort reform contend that our penchant for suing one another drives up the cost of health care, limits access to health care, scares away business, suppresses job creation, and hinders economic growth. Opponents counter that the level of litigation in the United States is not too high, and greed drives those who do very well financially from accepting any culpability if their pursuit of wealth injures or harms an individual or group of individuals.

Both arguments are worthy of consideration and for some they even lead to visceral responses. As such, civil litigation is a routinely politicized justice issue. States have undertaken reform of the civil systems, and the federal government recently reformed class action lawsuits. Doctors claim that exorbitant malpractice insurance premiums are prohibiting them from practicing medicine. They collectively lobby Congress for reforms, picket outside clinics, and close their practices to make political statements about the need for reform. Other organized interest uses equal or greater tactics. This chapter examines tort law in the United States in an effort to answer the question: are we too litigious? What is the standard by which litigation levels can be compared? Does civil litigation slow down the courts, drive up insurance costs, scare off business, and make it difficult for the United States to compete globally? Have efforts of reform been premature and too politicized? Has justice been undermined by the politicization of tort law?

Torts and Justice

Even passive observers of the civil justice system are aware of the case involving the plaintiff who sued McDonalds when she spilled hot coffee on herself which caused severe burns. Her award of millions of dollars rattled the business community, created late night fodder on the comedy circuit, and gave reformists all the ammunition needed to make the case symbolic of the ignorance, greed, and irrational nature of the civil justice system.[1]

Regardless of the decision in the "McCoffee" case, the ability to bring cases to court when one is harmed is a fundamental civil right. The Constitution guarantees both natural and civil rights. Neither can be denied without due process. Embodied in the Constitution's Seventh Amendment, "(I)n Suits at common law, where the value in controversy shall exceed twenty dollars, the right of trial by jury shall be preserved, and no fact tried by a jury, shall be otherwise re-examined in any Court of the United States, than according to the rules of the common law," the Framers of the Constitution realized that the ability to seek redress on civil matters was as important as due process in criminal matters.[2]

Even with the perceived equal weight of both civil and criminal law, within the legal system there are notable differences. These distinctions provide the limitations of civil justice and are therefore important. Civil justice deals with private wrongs originating between individuals, corporations,

---

[1] *Liebeck v. McDonalds Corp.*(1995) She was originally awarded $2.9M which was reduced by the judge in the case to around $650,000. She later settled with McDonalds for an undisclosed amount.

[2] For a concise discussion of trial by jury in civil cases see FindLaw article at the following web address: http://caselaw.lp.findlaw.com/data/constitution/amendment07/01.html#1.

and government. Cases are brought to trial by individuals, and in some cases, the states. In criminal matters, it is the responsibility of the state to pursue violations of criminal law. Civil cases don't involve incarceration or defamation associated with criminal violations. Typically, procedural standards are less formal and the threshold of a finding of fault is lower.[3]

Areas of civil litigation are fairly mundane: contract disputes, divorce cases, product liability, medical malpractice, and property questions comprise most civil cases. Landlords sue over rent payments. Neighbors dispute property lines. Deformed faces sue plastic surgeons. Homeowners who are unhappy with a contractor's work sue in small claims court. All of these vague descriptions have formed the substance of civil cases. Civil litigation can range from the mundane to the unique, serious to laughable, and illegitimate to serious. Advocates of reform tend to latch on to the aberrant cases. Resistors don't give legitimacy to complaints.[4]

Damages and Harm

Most of the disagreement over civil liability centers on the notions of harm and reasonable compensation for damages. Two kinds of monetary awards are common in civil cases. Compensatory damages supposedly compensate a harmed individual for the actual costs of the harm suffered. The intent of compensatory damages is to make an individual "whole." Punitive damages provide most of the controversy in tort law. How much is a life worth? What monetary award would deter

---

[3] In civil matters, the scope is much broader and less restrictive. Instead of reasonable doubt the threshold for fault is preponderance of the evidence.

[4] After the McDonalds coffee case, fictitious civil cases were circulated around the Internet called Stella Awards. Another group countered with True Stella Awards that described actual cases. www.stellaawards.com

a company from intentionally defrauding the government out of taxes owed to it? How much would be required to prohibit drug manufacturers from rushing their products to market when they know the risks of exposure to the drug are lethal?[5]

Before we get into the politics of tort reform, we need to boil away the material that clouds the discussion. Economic activity requires an interaction between mankind, as well as humanity and machinery. During this interaction, people are injured. Sometimes the injuries are severe, others are minor. Our legal system allows redress of harm in the courts. So our issue becomes what to do with those who are harmed. In the end we have injury and a right to hold those who injure us accountable. By examining a couple of areas of civil law, medical malpractice and product liabilty, we can see how tort cases have developed over time. We can then look at society's response via reform efforts. Through both, we clearly observe the politics of tort law.

Medical Malpractice

Early in (2005), United States President George W. Bush called for a federal law that would limit the prevalence of what he called "junk lawsuits" that drive up the cost of health care.[6]

---

[5] For examples of these cases see *Alabama v. Exxon* (1999) organized an intentional system of defrauding the State of Alabama from royalty payments. Company memos bragged about the ability to use accounting measures that would shield the amount owed. They contended that the folks in Alabama did not have the ability to figure out the complex scheme. Merck recently suffered after the Food and Drug Administration pulled the drug. Discovered company trials revealed that they knew of high risks in some patients, yet proceeded [with bringing the product to market.

[6] President's Proposed Remedy to Curb Medical Malpractice Lawsuits Stalls Senate Deadlocks; Democrats Plan To Use Filibuster , Jeffrey H. Birnbaum & John F. Harris, Washington Post Staff Writers Sunday, April 3, 2005; p. A05.

Bush's proposal was a classic tort reform issue aimed at shielding doctors and hospitals from large malpractice awards. His plan sought caps on pain and suffering awards, stretches payouts over time, and limits the length of time malpractice claims can be filed from the actual injury.

Without these protections, the President claimed that health care costs would continue to rise, malpractice premiums would run doctors out of business, and access to health care would be limited. In the (2005) State of the Union, in order to make sure health care remains viable, the President asserted that we must have "medical liability reform that will reduce health care costs and make sure patients have the doctors and care they need."[7]

Reformers also argue that without tort reform doctors will alter their care techniques and practice "defensive medicine" that will further increase the cost of health care. Defensive medicine results in an overabundance of diagnostic tests in order to ward off the possibility of a malpractice finding.[8] Thus, the potential health care problems that will only get worse without civil litigation reform include poor care, fewer doctors, rising costs, and injustice stemming from frivolous lawsuits. These are essentially the political arguments proffered by those advocating reform. No doubt, frivolous cases are filed, and they must be excluded from the system. We contend that "junk" lawsuits are rare which leaves us with the other assertions made by reform advocates.

Empiricism v. Politics

President Bush's assertions don't have to be taken at face value. Several government offices such as the Congressional

---

[7] State of the Union 2005. The White House. http://www.whitehouse.gov/news/releases/2005/02/20050202-11.html

[8] www.medterms.com

Budget Office, General Accounting Office, Office of Technology Assessment, and the Department of Health and Human Services have examined the proposals for reforming medical malpractice at the federal level based upon almost three decades of experiences in the states. Very little empirical evidence exists to support the claims of medical malpractice reformists.

The Congressional Budget Office examined the total cost of medical malpractice claims in relation to the overall cost of health care in the United States and found that malpractice claims amounted to approximately 2% of the total cost of health care consumption.[9] Part of the proposed reform would place caps on non-economic damages, as well as shift some costs that would result in no net medical savings, thus reducing malpractice insurance liability by roughly a fourth. This would result in a net health care savings of around .5 percent of the total cost spent on health care.[10] No conclusive evidence exists that demonstrates whether malpractice torts account for any significant portion of health care.

Defensive medicine is an additional issue raised by reformists. They contend that doctors order additional tests and procedures in order to ward off possible lawsuits for not aggressively treating patients' concerns. The most comprehensive examination to date on defensive medicine found no significant link between malpractice threats and defensive medicine.[11] Scattered research has found some small relationships between malpractice and defensive techniques in very narrow fields of medicine that typically are not

---

[9] Congressional Budget Office, Limiting Tort Liability for Medical Malpractice, January 8, 2004.

[10] CBO estimates that health care spending totaled 1.4 trillion in 2002, see note 9.

[11] Harvard Medical Study (1990) Patients, Doctors, and Lawyers, Medical Injury, Malpractice Litigation, and Patient Compensation in New York, Harvard University School of Public Health, Boston, MA.

reproducible in other areas.[12] We can not therefore conclude that all defensive medicine is related to torts, but could be attributed to income and the psychological well being of the patient. Conscientious physicians may also err on the side of caution and have no reference for possible tort claims. At best, defensive medicine claims for tort reform are overstated.

Potential malpractice suits are supposed to drive away individuals from the medical profession. The General Accounting Office analyzed the claim that malpractice torts hindered the availability of physicians. The GAO essentially confirmed a pattern of low access in areas where one would expect to find few specialized physicians: rural areas and obstetrics, primarily. Doctors simply are not drawn to rural areas where pay is low, and culture is homogenized. With student loans, relationship pressures, and lifestyle considerations, the lack of doctors in certain areas of the United States is more attributable to the unsuitable living conditions and not malpractice claims. Moreover, applications to medical schools and the number of physicians continue to increase. Their choice of location and specialty has virtually no link to malpractice.[13]

Earlier we asserted that the claim that our courts are filled with junk lawsuits were rare has also been borne out by empirical research. In a (1991) study of New York Hospitals, researchers found that only 1.5% of all medical malpractice instances resulted in a claim.[14] Not all were successful, either. It seems that negligent errors are often not pursued in the

---

[12] Daniel Kessler & Mark McClella, "Do Doctors Practice Defensive Medicine?" Quarterly Journal of Economics, (1996) May, pp.353-90. Their study found mixed results for reform.

[13] GAO Report, Medical Malpractice: Implications of Rising Premiums on Access to Health Care, GA)-03-836, (2003).

[14] Localio, et al (1991). Relation Between Malpractice Claims and Adverse Events Due to Negligence, New England Journal of Medicine. Vol. 325, no 4, pp. 245-51.

courts. These findings are consistent with research on the decision to seek redress in courts between those who have the ability and motivation to pursue a tort, and those who may have few resources and knowledge of the legal process.[15]

Very few political claims related to medical malpractice are rooted in any empirical reality. This area of tort law serves as prima facie evidence that it is easier to demagogue an issue rather than propose solutions that protect patients and others who are harmed by negligence. In a just society, all negligence would be punished. We account for approximate 1% of all harm done. Yet, somehow, the low probability of being sued for malpractice is not enough for elite citizens such as physicians. As we alluded in chapter 2, policies are made by the elite for the elite, not for the masses who are blamed for rising health care costs.

Product Liability

In early (2005), General Motors spokesperson, Chris Preuss stated that "tort reform is a high agenda item for us." Product liability and medicine malpractice are driving substantial costs into the system and making it more difficult for manufacturers to compete globally and create jobs." We have already debunked the myth that health care costs are significantly impacted by tort law, but the claim that torts hurt job creation and global competitiveness are also worth examining. As Dye contends, liberal and conservative elite both have a single goal of economic growth. Anything that threatens this growth must be stamped out of existence.

Reformists have taken aim primarily at the current asbestos litigation that is tied up in Congress. The total liability associated with those payouts could be around $300 billion. Their efforts are at work in both the federal and state

---

[15] See Divided Legal Profession, and One Shotters and Repeat Players.

levels. Elite interest groups, such as the American Tort Reform Association and the National Association of Manufacturers, are involved.[16] They contend that the tort system in the United States is a system that is dysfunctional, irrational, and abusive to taxpayers and business.

In (1990), Director of Income Security Issues for the GAO, Joseph Delfico, testified before Congress that most torts in product liability cases resulted in awards to those injured that were "strongly associated with the severity of the injury and, presumably, the plaintiff's underlying economic losses."[17] His examination also found that million dollar verdicts were rare, and additional studies had concluded that if anything, severely injured victims were "under compensated."[18] Deflico also testified that punitive damages were typically related to the size of the compensatory damages; rarely did they exceed the limits of caps that have been in place in other jurisdictions, and in most cases, the award was reduced upon appeal or post trial negotiation.

The GAO also reported in the same (1990) testimony that it appeared to them that juries carefully weighed the actions of the defendants against the standards of negligence even in strict liability cases. It seems juries discharge their duties conscientiously in civil matters. One troubling area was confirmed by the GAO's examination: time. On average, civil cases take over two years to process through the court system. Stalling has become a tactic of those who are negligent, which

---

[16] Former Michigan Governor heads up the National Association of Manufacturers. He has been a staunch supporter of reform since his time as governor. He has also formed a partnership with the American Justice Partnership headed up by former political allies.

[17] Joseph Delfico. Product Liability: The Tort System in Five States, GAO Director's Statement before the Committee on Commerce, Science, and Transportation, United States Senate. The quote can be found on page 4 of GAO/T-HRD-90-14.

[18] Id.

causes loss of evidence, injustice, and drives up costs. Over half of the costs in civil cases are legal fees.[19] These cases do represent time consuming and costly problems for the justice system.

Delfico's testimony in (1990) both uncovered and confirmed many of the "facts" associated with product liability specifically and the tort system in general. His conclusion that reform efforts are difficult to measure accurately is significant for our discussion. We have contended that much of the tort reform discussion is more ideologically and politically driven than the facts would warrant. As Delfico concluded, reformists would continue to push for changes that would make the tort system more beneficial to business. Only fifteen short years later, we have federal reforms aimed at Deflico's criticisms.

In early (2005), President George W. Bush signed the Class Action Fairness Act of 2005. The Act is "a practical way to begin restoring common sense and balance to America's legal system… (and a way to) ease the needless burden of litigation on every American worker, business, and family," said President Bush.[20] The aim of CAFA 2005 was to move most class action suits into the federal court system thereby preventing jury shopping. It was also supposed to protect injured persons from receiving insignificant awards for actual damages. Some class action suits result in very small awards for the injured while the attorneys make handsome paydays.[21]

Opponents of the reform contend that the real intent of CAFA 2005 was to limit the number of class action lawsuits in

---

[19] Id.

[20] President George W. Bush. The White House. "The President Signs Class Action Fairness Act of 2005. www.whitehouse.gov/news/releases/20052/02/print/20050218-11.html.

[21] Anecdotal evidence include cases where people were involved in class action lawsuits but were unaware of it, award checks for a few pennies, and some were given additional faulty merchandise by the same manufacturer.

the legal system not out of any real desire to make the system more efficient, but rather to diminish the likelihood that cases would be combined and brought together. Important to their cause, the federal courts have been the least hospitable venue for class action cases. Thus, they contend, cases that previously had merit will probably no longer be pursued.

An additional point of contention is that CAFA 2005 is just a down payment on future legal reforms. In his signing ceremony, the President did not hide his approval of reform, or his desire that the CAFA law become "important progress" toward "more to do" so that "small business owners across America" won't have to fear "one junk lawsuit", and "medical liability" won't continue to drive "up the cost for doctors and patients and entrepreneurs around the country. He also included Asbestos legal reforms measures that are currently in Congress because asbestos claims have "led to bankruptcy of dozens of companies and cost tens of thousands of jobs, even though many asbestos claims are filed on behalf of people who aren't actually sick," the President added.[22]

CAFA 2005 will probably be the initial step in reforming our tort laws to make them friendlier to the negligent. Much tort reform has already occurred in the states, and those efforts are worth examining to highlight some of the politics associated with these issues. Asbestos was mentioned previously. Currently, legislation is winding its way through Congress that will benefit one party or the other. When all of the smoke, fog, and politics are cleared, one thing remains: tort reform is touted as a panacea for a problem we don't even know exists for certain. We will briefly examine some state reform efforts, and what they mean for average citizens and business.

---

[22] See Supra note 20.

State Reforms

Through legislation in (1999), The State of Alabama enacted tort reform. Advocates of reform claimed Alabama's national reputation as a place known for jackpot justice and tort hell hurt economic development and suppressed job growth. Some of the highlights of the reform included: caps on punitive damages of $500,000 or three times compensatory damages when no physical injury is present; cap on punitive damages of $1.5 million or three times compensatory damages when physical injury occurred, and protections for small businesses.[23]

Reformists contend that before these changes took effect, Alabama was hindered from attracting small business, big business, or helping existing business to expand. Economic development officials contend that tort reform was the leading issue when the state sought to expand its automobile manufacturing base. Honda located a plant in Lincoln, AL shortly after tort reform was passed. The plant employs thousands of workers, and its ancillary suppliers have also created significant numbers of jobs in smaller communities in Alabama and the surrounding states.

Most recently, Alabama was ranked as an ideal business climate. Site selection, an economic development trade publication, recognized Alabama for its labor, land, workforce training, and abundance of natural resources.[24] While tort reform did occur before many of these economic successes happened, many reformists would contend that without these

---

[23] Alabama Policy Institute, Guide to Issues: Tort Reform. Alabamapolicy.org.

[24] Siteselection.com. and Mark Arend (May, 2005). Alabama Claims the Prize.

reforms, Alabama would not have the success it is now enjoying.

In other areas where economic and legal activity intersects, Alabama law allows legal remedies such as mandatory arbitration. Corporations have been using arbitration for years, but Alabama insurance companies can now refuse to issue policies to anyone who does not agree to have disputes settled by mediators. Mandatory and binding arbitration essentially requires consumers of insurance to waive their constitutional right to trial by jury in civil matters. Companies win as legal fees and settlement costs are lowered by not having to engage in lengthy court battles. Advocates of binding arbitration contend that the system is better for those who suffer injury as cases are resolved quicker than in traditional tort systems. The idea for mandatory arbitration did not originate with consumers. We contend the insurance companies enjoy the advantage, as it is not fathomable that they would advocate for changes that diminish their ability to compete in the market place.[25]

Michigan

Michigan's product liability laws, enacted under the leadership of former Governor John Engler, are considered to be potentially a national model for tort reform.[26] In (1995) the Michigan Legislature enacted a series of product liability that substantially modified tort cases in this area. Some of the more significant provisions included the elimination of joint liability, caps on damages, standards of evidence,

---

[25] Not all insurance companies in Alabama use binding arbitration. Some even realize there is a negative stigma attached to forcing consumers to sign mandatory arbitration agreements.

[26] Freep.com. A Michigan law stirs a national debate March 1, 2005. Patricia Anstett and Kim Norris.

admissibility of expert testimony, and eliminating tort cases for products that meet federal regulations such as prescription drugs. This latter issue is one that recently rattled the tort system.

One of Michigan's product liability reforms was aimed at curbing lawsuits over faulty prescription drugs. MCLA 600.2946 states that the manufacturer or seller of a drug may not be found liable if the drug was approved by the United States Food and Drug Administration. Recently, makers of some prescription drugs such as Vioxx have been sued everywhere but in Michigan. As an FDA approved drug, Michigan exempts the manufacturer or retailer of the product from liability. Former Governor Engler who heads the National Association of Manufacturers contends that the law is sane and fair since states should not be able to second guess the FDA.[27]

It could be years before the truth is known about how some drugs (proven to be safe) ultimately enter the market and harm consumers. Stephen Ceccoli has written a concise piece of research that clearly demonstrates the politicized and consumer driven process of drug marketing and approval.[28] With the growing medicated population in the United States, consumers of drugs will want to insure they are taking safe medications. We know some drugs will be harmful. Laws like Michigan's don't square with the flawed drug regulatory policies currently in place. Ceccoli reminds us that deference to a regulatory agency can be at our own peril. Advocates of wholesale liability reform can indeed look to Michigan for a strong model of reform. They can also see where harm is possible particularly in the area of drug sale and manufacturing. Negligence and harm can occur even with regulatory oversight.

---

[27] Id.

[28] Stephen Ceccoli & Pill Politics: Drugs and the FDA. Lynne Reiner: CO.

Mississippi

In (2004), the State of Mississippi enacted legislation that has been hailed as "winning the tort war."[29] Some pretty standard reforms were achieved including establishing venue for each plaintiff, elimination of joint liability, caps on damages, and excusing sellers and distributors if they did not know a product was faulty.[30] These reforms are considered extraordinary for a state that had been labeled by the American Tort Reform Association as a "judicial hellhole" and hotbed for jackpot justice.[31]

Reformists contend they were successful due to a confluence of events that created an unstoppable. New executive leadership in Mississippi from Governor Haley Barbor and Lt. Governor Amy Tuck both ran on reform platforms, and both won their seats with safe margins. Shortly after becoming governor, Barbour called a special session that swept in the aforementioned product liability cases. They contend that reform is just common sense.[32] What then might be the repercussions of reform in Mississippi? Obviously, it is too early to tell, but Mississippi does provide an interesting case for further elaboration.

The politics of tort reform vary from locale to locale. National reform advocates have rightly placed most of their efforts at the state level where legislators are factionalized, and interest group activities are more intense, the likelihood for reform is greatest in those states with ideologies that are

---

[29] Winning the Tort War in Mississippi: Keys for Success in other States. Charles Ross, State Senator, (2004). American Tort Reform Association. www.atra.org

[30] Id.

[31] Atra.org.

[32] See Supra note 29.

closer aligned to reform. In Mississippi, a conservative state with pro-business leadership, it is not surprising that significant reforms were enacted that create a pro-growth atmosphere for business expansion. As competitors with Alabama, and we have noted Alabama's successes, Mississippi used the politics of money as a reform issue. After tort reform took place in Mississippi, many reformists were probably relieved. In essence reforms aimed at curbing tort claims are common sense to them. We, however, don't believe the answer is that clear and we are left with our original question: Are we in the United States overly litigious? We still don't have enough information to answer that question clearly. Despite the certainty of politicians, we are not convinced that we are an overly litigious society. By examining some of the common statistics used in tort reforms and comparative public policy, we can begin to answer the question of whether we are too litigious, if the rush to reform is warranted and if the politics are meaningful.

Litigious Society?

On the surface, some of the stronger arguments for tort reform seem very valid. The United States has the most lawyers of any other country, and the growth of the legal profession has been greater than population growth over the past three decades.[33] Thus, there exists a steady supply of legal capacity to pursue tort claims. Civil cases have increased at a rate that eclipses the growth of all other cases filed. The result of this litigious appetite costs money and creates injustices. Total tort law equates to roughly 2% of the U.S. economy which is

---

[33] Richard Sander & Douglass Williams (1989). Why are there so many Lawyers? Perspectives on a Turbulent Market, Law and Social Inquiry. Vol. 14, no 3, pp 431-79.

double of the second country.[34] Brookings revealed that the cost of an automobile includes $500 attributable to tort cases.[35] Using Insurance Information Institute Data, the Public Policy Institute of New York estimated that the "tort tax" costs a family of four over $2,400 through inflated costs for medical care, cars, ladders, and vaccines.[36]

If these "facts" had to be taken at face value, we should probably move forward with a repeal of the Seventh Amendment to the Constitution. For example, product advertising is roughly equitable to the costs associated with tort protection. Some of the counter arguments to the notion of "tort taxes" i.e. closed businesses and injustice are meritorious as well. The most damage to the litigious argument is that tort awards over the past decades have not increased. Essentially, we have a "tort breakdown" myth not borne of empirical analyses.[37] Additionally, medical malpractice claims have also stayed relatively flat in relation to the overall size of the health care economy. We also know, as established earlier, that not every injured person seeks damages in courts. Tort cases make up a small percentage of court cases. It may very well be that the "system is working correctly". According to David S. Casey Jr., President of the Association of Trial Lawyers of America, "the whole effort by what I call the tort reform industry is based on myth and fabrication."[38] We believe that the reality of tort law in the United States falls somewhere between two oppositional views to the question: Are we a litigious society?

---

[34] Engler. National Association of Manufacturers

[35] Brookings.org

[36] Ppinys,org. These estimates are from 1996. Current estimates place the "tort tax" at approximately $3,200 per family of four.

[37] "Attorney Fees in Class Action Settlements: An Empirical Study" (with Geoffrey P. Miller), 1 Journal of Empirical Legal Studies 27-78 (2004).

[38] Jonathan Galanter (January 14, 2004). New York Times. Cornell Study Debunks Corporate Myth of Lawsuit Explosion.

Summary

Determining whether or not the United States is an overly litigious society is not as easy a proposition as politicians, interest group lobbyists, and pundits would have us believe. Foremost, we don't have reliable and valid measures of litigiousness. Most cited measures isolate one aspect of the tort economy without relating it to other variables known to effect torts. Concrete multivariate analysis is virtually non-existent. What is known for certain is that individuals are harmed when their interactions become as numerous as they are in a global economy based on information and services. Several thorough histories of tort law exist that are virtually divorced from political discussions of civil litigation.[39]

While it has been alluded to earlier, we feel it is important to contend that the United States is not an overly litigious society. The argument also flows from our theoretical framework. Not everyone who is harmed ultimately pursues his or her case in court. Studies have shown that anywhere from around 1% in medical malpractice cases to around 10% in product liability cases actually pursue their cases in court. Thus, we have a theoretical expectation that only those who have the legal skill and resources to pursue compensation will do so. We have some scholars who assert that a dichotomy exists in the legal profession known as "divided legal profession."[40] Essentially the legal profession is divided among those "elite" lawyers and firms who represent government, corporations, and the wealthy. The rest of the legal community represents everyone else. Essentially, we

---

[39] Divorce is the largest contributor to the United States growth of civil cases. Asbestos claims account for most product liability case loads.

[40] John Heinz & Edward Laumann (1982). Chicago Lawyers: The Structure of the Bar. Sage Publications.

have lawyers for the wealthy and powerful, and lawyer for the masses.

Coupling the scholarship of the divided legal profession with the scholarship on legal strategies related to suing shows a bleak picture to individuals harmed by medical malpractice and damaging products. Marc Galanter has established a dichotomy that spells trouble for tort justice of the masses.[41] Galanter distinguishes between those who are repeat players (RP) and one shotters (OS). Repeat players are those oriented in business and significant economic activity. One shotters would be those who have custody disputes, divorce, property squabbles with a neighbor, or issues with family. As one might expect, repeat players in the legal system routinely fair better than those who have marginal experience with the legal system. Repeat players develop legal strategies, maintain affiliations with those in the upper echelon of the legal profession, and calculate legal costs as a part of doing business. One shotters are not that savvy, and do not fare nearly as well in the process. Their behavior is indeed not strategic.

---

[41] Marc Galanter (1974). Why the Haves Come Out Ahead: Speculations on the Limits of Legal Change. Law and Society Review, Vol. 9. pp. 95-160.

Chapter Ten Summary

Justice in the United States is divided unevenly between those who have money and political power, and those who are less affluent. No great societal benefit is derived from this fact except to maintain power and affluence of those who have it. In the preceding chapters, we've tried to portray the justice system in the United States as working within a larger political apparatus dominated by the moneyed elite. No sinister intentions were levied by us. We are not opponents of law enforcement, judges, or any public servant—elected or appointed. Our overriding goal for this treatise was to create a better understanding of the pursuit of justice for students and citizens alike. Perhaps we've been successful.

Justice polices—get tough on crime, three-strike laws, war on drugs—are elite driven policies that have not resulted in reduced crime. Their only purpose is to stoke the fears of the masses while allowing themselves to be portrayed as doing everything possible to protect society. Ultimately, a crime fearing society that must fund more prison construction, security personnel, police officers, drug agents, investigators, equipment purchases, and judges. Thus, we are left with drug epidemics, crowded court dockets, overworked police officers, and bloated prisons. Our justice policies simply don't work.[1]

The lack of comprehensive policies spells doom for our justice system? The primary consequences of failed policies are less than efficient justice administration. Here's how failed administration looks: an officer makes an arrest on minor drug charges that requires hours work not related to

---

[1] Robert Martinson levied the accusation that "nothing works" in regards to rehabilitation and crime reduction.

traditional police work, hours later (less than the officer will dedicate to the matter) the alleged criminal is at home on bond, he is not able to afford an attorney so the state must provide one, he is on probation so his probation officer is involved. His trial is set for three months later, and a continuance is granted for another three months. After six months, the state's attorney and state provided attorney strike a deal for a guilty plea on lesser charges to include a longer probation and drug treatment. The offender fails the treatment program and the cycle starts over with another chance and numerous visits with his probation officer. Much of the time the drug activity continues. Society's investment is wasted. Most importantly, the justice personnel—police, probation officers, attorneys, judges, treatment program—efforts are for nothing. Society does not get much of a return for its investment. Thus, failed administration is predicated on poorly developed drug control policy.

Failed policies and administration allows us to comfortably claim that the justice system is also failing. We don't maintain objectivity, continuity, or efficiency with the system.[2] Most of the time, the various components of the justice system are treated separately as if one branch's work did not influence the others. Obviously this is a flawed approach. When the police make arrests, the courts must deal with the alleged crimes. When courts administer a sentence, they are carried out in our corrections component. Incorrect punishment, flawed treatments programs, and incomprehensible sentencing patterns, along with plea bargaining, essentially signal the start of this cycle all over again. Thus, we have the components of a system, but they are not appropriately linked together through planning, coordination, and development. These conditions can be ameliorated with conscientious attention.

---

[2] See Matthew Robinson for this indictment.

Law Enforcement

Our discussion of law enforcement focused primarily on their use of discretion and political factors affecting socialization of officers to the profession. Police work is often politicized, and much of the criticism or complaint is exaggerated. Contemporary police work is marked by competing demands, cross pressures, and conflicting goals all within the environment of increased responsibility. Issues facing society and large also affect the work of police. For example, U.S. citizens are economically squeezed (especially among the typical offender demographic) and police agency budgets are limited. To compete in a global marketplace of ideas more education is needed. For police officers to cope within a borderless world, more education is needed. As the drug problem continues to plague society, law enforcement is asked to be a panacea. Modern law enforcement officers, to be successful, must be able to understand the legal, social, economic, and moral workings of society. Thus, a good police officer is expected to be very verse in many areas i.e. law, political science, sociology, psychology, theology, and economics. This combination of expertise makes police work one of the most demanding occupations of our time.

Terrorism has taken advantage of the information age. Information and communication has essentially shut down borders and allowed access to countries a person would have never dreamt of seeing. Those tasked with managing threats and responding to the acts of terrorism are our first responders—police, fire, EMT. The specter of terrorism places additional burdens on our law enforcement officers including the protection of critical infrastructure, coordinating information concerning potential terrorism, and reacting in the event of a catastrophe. These additional responsibilities require more training, equipment, expertise, and understanding of local law enforcement's place within a growing national law enforcement paradigm. On the whole, government has been slow to provide our law enforcement officers the necessary support needed to meet the needs of increased threats and complex demands.

Law enforcement has sought to meet some of the challenges it faces through changing the way departments are organized. Over the past generation of officers, we've seen emphases placed on greater levels of professionalism, standardization, education, and responsiveness to citizens through a morphing organization structure. Like many others, we believe law enforcement and the community are synonymous terms. Thus, the growth of community policing whereby citizens are encouraged to communicate and share in the process of law enforcement has somewhat improved crime rate, pressures on law enforcement, and community satisfaction. In areas where community policing has been given lip service, not much has changed except who funds police operations.

Law enforcement can see the politicized nature of its work diminish through more open operations and communication with citizens. There are simply too many demands on law enforcement for their work not to be conducted in partnership with the community. Experience has shown us that law enforcement is most successful when aided by the citizenry. Community policing embodies a philosophical shift that captures this fact. Instead of interacting with citizens at arms length, which provides an opportunity for politicizing law enforcement's work, the cooptation of community sentiments will less politics and enhance the success of society's police function.

Courts

Many of the provisions guaranteed by the Constitution are empty promises in U.S. courts. Most cases i.e. 95% are plea bargained. For those who go to trial, the process is slow and unpredictable. Widespread access to top notch legal counsel is not a reality. Punishments are erratic. On the surface, there does not appear to be much justice in the court process. The question we must consider is what differences would materialize if legal access were more egalitarian, trials more efficient, and punishment proportional to the crime.

Good evidence exists that those who have the means to fight for their rights and interests in court do better than those with limited means. Anecdotal evidence is also strong for the argument that legal acumen usually delivers the legal outcomes sought by the wealthy, connected, and powerful. This evidence exists despite the fact that crimes committed by the wealthy, powerful, and connected cost society more than street crime by over six fold. Crime in the streets versus suites is a matter of which defendant has the ability to defend his or her actions in court. Those engaged in white collar crime most recently have done little or no time, and paid fines that are a pittance of what shareholders, insurance companies, and their own businesses lost during their piracy. Richard Scrushy, former HealthSouth executive, was found not guilty of leading a scheme to overstate his company's profits during the heyday of 1990's. Enron executives have not been punished severely or on a wide scale for monopolistic practices, cheating on their taxes, or exaggerating profits. Their misdeeds destroyed the lives of their employees and shook the equities market. Billions of dollars were lost when the Enron house of cards fell. Ken Lay, the leader of Enron, claimed he had no idea the fraud took place. In a 2004 editorial in the Washington Post, Lay claimed his prosecution was "political."[3] We have trouble imagining a drug dealer getting the opportunity to write a ripping accusation against the Justice Department for the Washington Post. Scrushy and Lay are not the only CEO's to face the wrath of the Justice Department but they do represent those who fought back and held their own. Martha Stewart committed few transgressions than either Scrushy or Lay, but was quickly indicted, tried, sentenced, and paroled. Her punishment, by most accounts, was nothing more than a slap on the wrist.

Uneven punishment or none at all for the wealthy undermines the credibility of the judicial process. Justice is also lost. As Martin Luther King reminded us, injustice anywhere is a threat to justice every where. Justice does not exist in some places and not in others. Justice can only exist when it is dispersed universally or at least pursued universally. Unfortunately, the courts show deference to those with resources. We don't think this is intentional, but rather a function of skill and ability. The court process is not different than most other processes: the success of failure of the process depends on relationships. Wealthy, powerful, and skilled court participants have those relationships that have been cultivated over a number of years. What we could do differently in terms of universal treatment by the courts is a complex process.

Expanded capacity may assist in distributing justice. More judges, clerks, technology, layers of bureaucracy could add the handling capacity that moves justice more swiftly. Better legal representation for everyone could iron out the

---

[3] Ken Lay (September 1, 2004). The Politics of My Trial. p. A19. In fairness to Mr. Lay, it does seem as if government officials have a publicly displayed distaste for him. Their rabid pursuit of him has not yielded the public a conviction yet, over four years after alleged misdeeds.

discrepancies that cause trouble for sentencing. Greater scrutiny of the judicial process could open up the deliberations, tactics, and machinations of the court beyond a media dramatized version of Court TV. The best disinfectant is sunshine. We propose stripping away the ostentatious appearance of the courts which is supposed to symbolize the place of law in society. Law, if applied fairly, takes the place as the binder of citizens in a social contract. When the legal process fails to hold accountable those who do the most harm to society, the law no longer binds us. The rule of law must be administered in an equitable, purposeful and meaningful way if we are to have justice.

Corrections

Corrections wield very little clout in the political process. Prisons ultimately are responsible for incarcerating inmates. Probation officers are given few tools to keep their cases on a law abiding path. There have not been enough investments in expanding the comprehensive range of punishments that reside between prison and probation.[4] Those in the corrections component of the justice system are left to deal with overcrowded prisons which are often the worst environments for work and living anywhere in the United States. Corrections is expensive for society. Not only do prisons have to be built, but staffed and maintained. Prisoners need feeding, medical care, recreation, and treatment. All of this takes money.

Resources are stretched in many states, and several competing demands exist for the few resources available to lawmakers. Thus, state and local governments find themselves struggling to take care of swelling correctional populations caused primary by politicized punishment.

[4] Some are starting to realize this is needed.

While the correctional departments don't make the laws, they do, however, have to manage the result of "getting tough" on crime, and waging "war" on various criminal elements of criminal activity. This raises the ultimate problem of politicized justice: those responsible for pressuring the justice system to do more aren't necessarily willing to pay for it. This fact leads to more politicization of the problem which is usually manifested in making prison sentences lengthy.

Society would benefit more from a more thoughtful punishment and treatment paradigm than currently exists. Thoughtfulness would include a thorough review of our drug control and crime policies. Perhaps it would include a decriminalizing of some drugs, but that is not entirely clear to us. We may rethink punishment orientations for drug possession, and invest in treatment rather than incarceration. The focus of a thoughtful drug control policy should be the reduction of demand. Our war on drugs has done nothing for supply or price, and the work done on demand has been only half-hearted by lawmakers. It seems paradoxical to us that the most addictive and destructive drugs—alcohol and nicotine—are legal and thriving enterprises.

Conclusion

Despite the hard work of law enforcement officers, court personnel, and corrections officials, crime is still prevalent in the United States and the treatment of crime is asymmetrical. It seems that moneyed elites control justice policies, and the work of justice system personnel is politicized. The outcome of such tendencies is frequent injustice. We are not proposing the elimination of politics from the justice process because the suggestion is not plausible. Our aim here has been to describe the environment in which justice policies are developed, implemented, and evaluated. When justice decisions are politicized they usually fail out of accommodation for many different perspectives. Understanding the political environment is essential in understanding the justice system as a set of loosely tied together components.